ANNA JORDAN

Anna Jordan's play *Yen* won the 2013 Bruntwood Prize for Playwriting. Her other plays include *Freak* (Theatre503/ Edinburgh Festival Fringe); *The Freedom Light* (Company of Angels); *Closer to God* (Offcut Festival); *Stay Happy Keep Smiling* (Soho); *BENDER* (Old Red Lion); *Coming Home* (Bush); *Staunch* (Arcola); *Fragments* (Riverside) and *Just for Fun – Totally Random* (Lost One Act Festival). Her work as a director includes *Tomorrow I'll Be Happy* by Jonathan Harvey (National Theatre Shed, 2013 NT Connections Festival); *Crystal Springs* (Eureka, San Francisco); *Vote of No Confidence*, *Only Human* (Theatre503). She is Artistic Director of Without a Paddle Theatre, and teaches acting and playwriting.

Anna Jordan

CHICKEN SHOP

NICK HERN BOOKS

London

www.nickhernbooks.co.uk

A Nick Hern Book

Chicken Shop first published in Great Britain in 2014 as a paperback original by Nick Hern Books Limited, The Glasshouse, 49a Goldhawk Road, London W12 8QP in association with Park Theatre, London and Epsilon Productions

Cover image: Kim Hardy Photography; designed by Epsilon Productions

Designed and typeset by Nick Hern Books, London
Printed in Great Britain by Mimeo Ltd, Huntingdon, Cambridgeshire PE29 6XX

A CIP catalogue record for this book is available from the British Library

ISBN 978 1 84842 428 9

Chicken Shop was first performed at Park Theatre, London, on 2 September 2014. The cast was as follows:

HILARY	Angela Bull
HENDRIX	Jesse Rutherford
KATIE	Millie Reeves
LEKO	John Last
LUMINITA	Lucy Roslyn

Director	Jemma Gross
Designer	Florence Hazard
Lighting Designer	Sherry Coenen
Production Manager	Christopher Silvester
Assistant Director	Charlotte Marigot
Producer	Epsilon Productions
	www.epsilonproductions.co.uk

Park Theatre

Park Theatre is a theatre for London today. Our vision is to become a nationally and internationally recognised powerhouse of theatre.

★ ★ ★ ★ ★ **'A spanking new five-star neighbourhood theatre.'**
Independent

We opened in May 2013 and stand proudly at the heart of our diverse Finsbury Park community. With two theatres, a rehearsal and workshop space plus an all-day café-bar, our mission is to be a welcoming and vibrant destination for all.

We choose plays based on how they make us feel: presenting classics through to new writing, musicals to experimental theatre all united by strong narrative drive and emotional content. In our first year we presented twenty-five plays, including ten world premieres and two UK premieres, welcoming over a hundred and twenty-seven thousand visitors through our doors.

Highlights included *Daytona*, with Maureen Lipman, which toured nationally and recently transferred to the West End, and *Yellow Face*, which transferred to the National Theatre Shed.

'A first-rate new theatre in north London.' *Daily Telegraph*

In our second year we're looking forward to growing our audience base, forging partnerships internationally and continuing to attract the best talent in the industry. Through a range of creative-learning activities we're also working with all ages to nurture new audiences and develop the next generation of theatre practitioners.

To succeed in all of this ongoing support is of paramount importance. As a charity, with no public subsidy, none of this is possible without the help of our Friends, trusts and foundations and corporate sponsors. To find out more about us, our artistic programme and how you can support Park Theatre, please go to **parktheatre.co.uk**

Park Theatre, Clifton Terrace, London N4 3JP
020 7870 6876 | parktheatre.co.uk

Park Theatre Staff List

Artistic Director	Jez Bond
Executive Director	John-Jackson (JJ) Almond
Creative Director	Melli Bond
Development Director	Dorcas Morgan
Assistant to the Directors	Amy Lumsden
Operations Manager	Tom Kingdon
Theatre and Buildings Technician	Nikki Sutton
Press Relations	Kate Morley PR
Sales Supervisor	Melissa Parry
Duty House Managers	Raya Dibs
	Androulla Erotokritou
	Hannah Halden

Ambassadors
David Horovitch
Celia Imrie
Sean Mathias
Hattie Morahan
Tamzin Outhwaite

Associate Artists
Mark Cameron
Olivia Poulet
Sarah Rutherford (writer-in-residence)
Charlie Ward

Trustees
Frances Carlisle
Stephanie Dittmer
Nick Frankfort
Colin Hayfield
Rachel Lewis
Chris McGill
Leah Schmidt (Interim Chair)
Danielle Tarento
President – Jeremy James

With thanks to all of our supporters, donors and volunteers

Characters

HENDRIX, *sixteen, British*
HILARY, *forty-three, British*
KATIE, *twenty-seven, Australian*
LUMINITA, *twenty-four, Moldovan*
LEKO, *thirty-eight, Albanian*

Settings

*Hilary's living room: a dining table. A small two-seater sofa.
Coffee table. Earthy. Understated. Full of plants and ethnic
knick-knacks and with an absence of technology. Two doorways,
stage left leading to the front door, kitchen and bathroom, stage
right leading off to the bedrooms.*

*Luminita's room: a low, single bed covered with a threadbare
flowery bedspread, a tall window next to it. Luminita's things
under the bed. The heavy curtains are always closed. To the left
of the bed, an old wooden school chair. A waste-paper bin.*

*Hendrix's bedroom: a single bed. A small modest telly. Posters.
A couple of artistic prints on the wall but also general teenage
mess. A bit of a shitpit.*

Note on Text

A forward slash (/) indicates overlapping speech.

A dash (–) at the end of a line means the next line interrupts.

*This text went to press before the end of rehearsals and so may
differ slightly from the play as performed.*

ACT ONE

Scene One

HENDRIX, *awkward, kind-hearted, earnest, sits at the breakfast table dressed in school uniform. He has a seriously floppy haircut. He is reading* FHM *magazine, and it is open to some very big-titted ladies. He has cereal spoon midway to mouth and is fixated. He hears his mother coming and quickly stuffs* FHM *in his bag.* HILARY, *grounded, earthy, a little worn but idealistic, walks through stage-right door, brushing her hair, her bottom half-dressed, but wearing a large greying bra.*

HILARY. Morning!

HENDRIX (*almost under his breath*). Jesus Christ!

She passes straight through to the other door. He tentatively lifts FHM *back out of his bag.* KATIE, *sparky, stunning, hyper-sexual, enters stage left wearing the smallest of towels and another towel covering her hair. He hides* FHM *immediately again. She flicks his ear, playfully, hard.*

Ow!

She is gone. He glances back at the other door, goes to take FHM *but then gives up. He takes a bite of the cereal, grimaces. He picks up the packet.*

'Organic Peace Muesli'. '*Peace* Muesli'. Fuck.

HILARY *enters with an open shirt on and goes straight to a mirror on the fourth wall to do her minimal make-up. Throughout the scene she gets ready to go out.*

HILARY. What are you 'fucking' about?

HENDRIX. Nothing. It's just do you think we could try something *nice* for breakfast? Something that doesn't look like it's been swept out of a rabbit's cage?

HILARY. There's porridge or Amaranth Flakes if you don't want that –

HENDRIX (*reading*). 'Sugar-free, wheat-free, gluten-free, GMO-free' –

HILARY. Just have some toast then – !

HENDRIX. – Taste-free… Fun-free!

HILARY. We have intolerances in this house, okay?

HENDRIX. *I'm* not intolerant. I'd say I'm pretty *bloody* tolerant.

HILARY. Katie can't handle the gluten. She's bordering on coeliac.

HENDRIX. Bordering on maniac.

HILARY. Hey!

Beat.

HENDRIX. Mother, I'm a growing… man. I need sustenance.

HILARY. Exactly!

HENDRIX. What I mean is what about a bit of bacon or sausage once in a while?

HILARY. Very funny.

Beat. HILARY *looks over at* HENDRIX, *perturbed.*

Do you eat meat when you're away from home? (*Beat.*) Actually, don't answer that I don't want to know.

Beat. HENDRIX *goes back to looking at the packet.*

Jesus, when's this weather going to break? I'm sweltering.

HENDRIX. Why do you have to bring all this stuff back from the shop? Eugh. 'Dried prune powder' –

HILARY (*spins round*). Okay, Hendrix! You go to the supermarket and get whatever sugar-coated Kellogg's crap you fancy but you can bloody well pay for it yourself! And you'll be sorry. When your glycaemic index goes through the roof.

HENDRIX. Oh yeah I'll be fucking devastated, Mother!

HILARY. ENOUGH WITH THE FUCKS, HENDRIX!

Silence. She goes back to her make-up.

HENDRIX. God. What's wrong with you?

HILARY. I'm bleeding.

He puts down his spoon heavily.

HENDRIX. Jesus Christ!

HILARY. What?

HENDRIX. Do you have to say *that*, Mum? Can't you just –

HILARY. What? Use one of those ridiculous euphemisms? 'It's my time of the month', or 'I've got the painters in'.

HENDRIX. No you could / just say –

HILARY. Or 'I'm on the blob'– ?

HENDRIX. NO! You could just say 'I've got my period'. Like a normal person. Like a normal fucking person, Mother.

HILARY. ENOUGH with the FUCKS, Hendrix!

Pause. HENDRIX *butters himself a piece of toast.*

HENDRIX. So if I pay for the Kellogg's myself I can have it, right?

HILARY. If that's really what you want.

Beat.

HENDRIX. So if I pay for a PlayStation 4 can I have that?

HILARY. Oh not *again*! No!

HENDRIX. Why not? Same diff!

HILARY. You call yourself a feminist. Right?

HENDRIX. Yeah.

HILARY. Then do you really want to play a video game where you can pick up a prostitute, rape her, kill her and take your money back?

HENDRIX. That's just one game!

HILARY. It's violent, it's misogynistic –

HENDRIX. Yeah but, Mum –

HILARY. And I'm not discussing it any more.

HENDRIX. Anyway, is it really rape if –

HILARY. DO NOT EVEN GO THERE, HENDRIX!

HENDRIX. Hey, no, I'm not saying it's right I just… Oh forget it.

Pause. HENDRIX *sulks.*

What about the laptop then?

HILARY. We've got a laptop.

HENDRIX. My *own* laptop!

HILARY. Hendrix, play fair. I got you the TV, didn't I?

HENDRIX. Yep. (*So she can't hear.*) And it's a piece of shit.

HILARY. Do you know children spend an average of six hours a day hooked into some kind of screen? It zaps your soul. Warps it. I don't want that for you. I want you to / buck the trend.

HENDRIX. Buck the trend. Yeah. I get it, Mum.

HILARY. And apart from anything we can't afford it.

HENDRIX. I was thinking maybe I could get one… instead of going to Barcelona.

HILARY. But you have to go. It's part of your A level.

HENDRIX. Not really. I can do all the coursework for it while they're away. On my laptop.

HILARY. Why don't you want to go?

Beat.

HENDRIX. I don't really get along with the boys in my history group.

HILARY. Why?

HENDRIX. I don't know, do I? They're just stupid.

HILARY. What about Melvin?

HENDRIX. Melvin?

HILARY. That's the boy that played tennis with you and Meg, isn't it? Isn't he in your group?

HENDRIX. God no, Mother. He's not even in my year. We just see each other in breaks sometimes.

HILARY. Oh.

HENDRIX. It's a lot of money. I could get a laptop for less than you're paying for the trip. *Please*, Mum?

HILARY. I don't want you to miss out on cultural opportunities. And anyway, we're paying in weekly instalments.

HENDRIX. I just don't think I can be bothered. Spending a whole four days with them.

HILARY. Come on, Hen. Dalí Museum? La Fábrica? You're not going to miss out on all that because of a few immature boys, are you?

HENDRIX. No, I suppose.

HILARY. Good.

Beat. She does a big yawn.

HENDRIX. Tired?

HILARY. Yes I had a bit of a bad night.

HENDRIX. Didn't sound too bad from my room.

KATIE breezes in wearing a little shorts and T-shirt pyjamas set.

KATIE. Morning, peeps!

HENDRIX is about to bite into a bit of toast but KATIE snatches it out of his hand.

HENDRIX. Mother, did you see that?

KATIE. Oh chillax, Hen, it's only a slice of toast.

KATIE sits on the dining-room table and eats.

HILARY. What are your plans today, darling?

KATIE. Not sure yet.

HILARY. Paint?

KATIE. Maybe. Maybe paint.

HENDRIX. The hall could do with a couple of coats.

KATIE. Hilarious, Hendrix.

HILARY. Button it! Good for you, Kate. Back on the horse.

KATIE. Yeah. I might start a new one. (*Has a big stretch.*) Yep, rip a fresh bit of canvas.

HILARY. You should finish the old woman. It could be the centrepiece of the collection.

KATIE. Nuh.

HILARY. You should try and finish at least one, Kate.

KATIE (*snapping a little*). Hils, don't challenge me please. (*Beat.*) You know I've been blocked.

HILARY. Okay. Sorry.

KATIE. It's okay. I might have a big sort-out. Tidy up.

HILARY. Now there's an idea. Creativity breeds in a tidy space.

KATIE. Yup. Might spring-clean the studio.

HENDRIX. Spare room.

HILARY. Hendrix.

HENDRIX. Well, it is! You never let Meg call it her workshop when she had her motorbike stuff in there.

KATIE *does a little 'humph' at the mention of Meg.*
HILARY *clocks this.*

In fact you never stopped moaning about it. Now it's full of half-finished pictures of naked Aborigine women and suddenly it's 'her studio'.

HILARY. Don't be uncharitable.

HENDRIX. You wouldn't let me have a drum kit in there last year when I asked.

KATIE. You should count yourself lucky. Most teenage boys would kill to have a spare room full of half-naked women!

HENDRIX. Yeah but not with the sort of tits that you paint!

HILARY. Hendrix – !

HENDRIX. They're like spaniels' ears!

HILARY. Stop! Hendrix, Katie is a very talented artist in the middle of putting together a very important collection. We should feel privileged to be around her while she's doing that, and give her the space she needs. Okay? Champ?

HENDRIX (*sigh*). Okay.

Beat.

KATIE. Thanks, Hen. You're welcome any time you know. Come in and watch me work?

HENDRIX. I thought you always worked in the nude?

KATIE. Oh, yeah. Maybe not then.

HILARY (*to* HENDRIX). Shouldn't you be gone by now?

HENDRIX. No. I've got ages.

KATIE. Ooh ooh ooh I know what I was going to do today!

HILARY. What, love?

KATIE. I'm going to get a job!

HENDRIX. Doing what?

KATIE. Not sure yet, I've just decided I am going to get one.

HILARY. But what about your painting, darling?

KATIE. Oh just part-time. I think interacting with other humans might kickstart me. And I want to contribute to the house.

HILARY. Well, that would be welcome. What sort of thing?

KATIE. Search me. I put it out into the universe this morning. An answer will find its way to me, sooner or later.

HENDRIX (*incredulous*). Oh fuck off!

HILARY. Hendrix!

KATIE. Don't abuse me because I don't conform, Hendrix.

HILARY. Have some respect for Katie.

HENDRIX. Whatever.

HILARY. I think it's a great idea, love, I really do. Come here.

> KATIE *goes to her and* HILARY *takes her face in her hands and kisses her passionately.* HENDRIX *sighs audibly.*

KATIE (*looking down*). Baby! We gotta get you some new undies!

> HILARY *looks down and closes her shirt.*

HILARY. Oh. Yeah.

HENDRIX. Here.

> *He thrusts her the local paper which is on the table.*

KATIE. What's this?

HENDRIX. Jobs section at the back. See if one of those 'finds its way' to you.

KATIE. Ooh I don't want to work in Hounslow.

HENDRIX. Snob!

HILARY. There's Twickenham jobs in there too.

KATIE. Oh amaze-balls.

> HENDRIX *snorts.* KATIE *takes the paper and opens it at the back.* HENDRIX *begins trying to do his tie.*

HENDRIX. God it's so hot in this house!

HILARY. Are you coming straight home tonight, dude?

HENDRIX. Yep.

HILARY. I mean if you want to go round to someone's house, or whatever, I don't mind. So long as you send me a text. You can do that.

HENDRIX. Mum, when do I ever do that?

HILARY. Alright. But I don't want you just floating round the car park, like last week, like a paper bag in the wind or something.

HENDRIX. OKAY, MUM!

KATIE (*looking at the back of the paper*). Christ! I'd be alright if I wanted a job in a massage parlour.

HILARY. That's a great idea. You'd be a great masseuse, you've got a wonderful touch.

HENDRIX. Oh puke.

KATIE. Yeah but not in these places, Hils.

HILARY. Why not?

KATIE. They're all fucking brothels!

HILARY. Let's see.

She gives her the paper.

'*Honeyz Massage. Gorgeous Ladies. Girlfriend Experience. Central Hounslow.*' Jesus Christ, in the local paper!

KATIE. That's the world we're living in.

HILARY. Well, stop it please, I'd like to get off.

HILARY *chucks the paper down on the table.* HENDRIX *picks it up and glances at it.*

I don't think I'll manage dinner tonight. I've got a new supplier coming late.

HENDRIX. Don't worry about me. I'll have a Maccy D's.

HILARY. Hilarious, Hendrix.

KATIE. I'll do something. I'll do something with that tofu.

HENDRIX. Ooh yum yum.

KATIE. Hendrix, I think I've got something of yours.

KATIE *pulls her middle finger out of her shorts pocket and sticks it up at him.* HENDRIX *is fiddling with his tie.*

HENDRIX. Grow up.

HILARY. Katie, you hate cooking.

KATIE. Hate cooking. Love you. That's the difference.

Beat. KATIE *and* HILARY *embrace.* HENDRIX *clocks it.*

HENDRIX. God's sake!

HILARY. What is wrong with you, Hennie?

HENDRIX. I can't do this tie! And don't call me Hennie, Mother!

HILARY. And don't call me Mother, Hendrix. You make me sound geriatric. (*Looks at her watch.*) Shit, Katie, help him, can you? I'm going to be late – and so are you, dude!

HILARY *exits into the bathroom.* HENDRIX *backs away a little but* KATIE *firmly goes to him and starts to do the tie. Beat.*

KATIE. Hendrix, are you wearing aftershave?

HENDRIX. It's just Lynx.

Beat. Awkward.

KATIE. There. Super-smart.

HILARY *enters.*

HILARY. Hendrix, are you wearing Lynx?

HENDRIX (*weary*). Yes. Why?

While HILARY *talks to* HENDRIX, KATIE *spies the* FHM *in* HENDRIX's *bag. She steals it stealthily, and drops it down the side of the sofa.*

HILARY. The bathroom stinks of it. I don't like aerosols in this house.

HENDRIX. Mother, I'm sixteen. Dragging a skanky crystal across my armpits just isn't going to cut it.

HILARY. What about roll-on?

HENDRIX. What about it?

HILARY. Never mind. You need to leave for school right now.

HENDRIX. I'm going!

HENDRIX goes about tidying up his stuff and putting it into his bag. HILARY *grabs her bag and ruffles his hair.*

HILARY. Okay, champ. Love you.

HENDRIX. Yeah yeah.

HILARY. Say it!

HENDRIX. Love you!

HILARY. We never leave the house without saying it.

KATIE (*enjoying this*). Love you!

HILARY. Love you too!

They kiss. KATIE *wants to keep it going longer than* HILARY, *she is all aglow with love.*

Right. (*A little weary but triumphant.*) Another day!

She is gone. There is a slightly loaded pause. HENDRIX *takes his blazer off and puts his bag down, half-defiant but half-cautious, looking at* KATIE *to see her reaction.*

KATIE. What are you doing?

HENDRIX. I've just remembered it's not compulsory, first lesson.

KATIE. Oh pull the other one, Hen.

HENDRIX. It's Citizenship. No one goes.

KATIE. Not like you to skip class.

Beat. HENDRIX *shrugs.*

I'm kind of responsible for you here, dude.

HENDRIX. No you're *not.*

KATIE. Okay. Well, what's it worth?

HENDRIX. What?

KATIE. Do you wanna do something together? Eat some cookies? Build some bridges?

HENDRIX. I just wanna read in my room.

KATIE. We could watch something on your telly.

HENDRIX. Do you go in my room when I'm not here?

KATIE. Of course not, Hen! I mean only for *Loose Women*. Joke! Joke! Okay. Go in your room it's cool.

HENDRIX (*unsure*). Cheers.

He picks up his bag and gets ready to go. He notices that FHM is missing, puts his bag down on the floor and starts to search, taking a few things out. KATIE grabs FHM from the sofa, enjoying the game.

KATIE. Looking for this?

HENDRIX. Fuck's sake!

He moves towards her and tries to grab it back, she keeps snatching it back.

KATIE. Hendrix Bottomley, you dirty dog!

HENDRIX. Give that back.

KATIE. Your mum would go fucking nuts if she saw this.

HENDRIX. Katie, I'm warning you.

Throughout he follows her trying to grab it and she snatches it away.

KATIE (*leafing through*). Clearly objectifying women here, Hen. You're a tits man then, are ya?

HENDRIX. I just like the articles. About films and... and gadgets –

KATIE. I don't blame you. I love a good pair of tits. That's why I'm so lucky with your mum.

HENDRIX. God you are so *gross*!

KATIE. Face it, babes, we've both had a suck on them –

HENDRIX. Euuugh! Fuck off!

KATIE (*looking at it*). Hang on. Why is this page turned down? Oh my God! '*Taming the Pussy Cat. The thinking man's guide to making a girl cum.*'

She begins to laugh hysterically. HENDRIX *starts to put stuff back in his bag, getting ready to leave.*

'The Golden Rules of ORAL: When you're doing something right, her body will rise and writhe, she might tremble or shake, she'll get wetter and wetter.'

HENDRIX. Shut up!

KATIE. 'She'll moan, pant, scream, tell you to go harder harder HARDER! Grab your head and pull it into her, shout at you to drive your tongue deeper.'

HENDRIX. Fuck you!

HENDRIX *leaves as quickly as he can.* KATIE *calls after him.*

KATIE. Harder, Hendrix! HARDER!

The door slams. She is amused.

Ahh...

KATIE *continues to look through the magazine. She throws herself on the sofa.*

Scene Two

Lights still on KATIE. *Lights slowly fade up on* LEKO, *hefty, intense, a large energy, lying on the bed swigging from a bottle of Bell's. He holds an underwear brochure, and he looks at a page with some models in provocative poses and raunchy lingerie.* LUMINITA, *delicate, birdlike, broken, stands by the wall wearing a denim skirt and a vest with 'Sexy' on it in diamanté (some of the studs are missing). She also sports a pair of very high heels. She is posed provocatively and awkwardly: hands on hips, legs apart, hip raised to one side.* LEKO *watches her.*

LEKO. Your hip, your hip should be out a little more, Luminita. Good. And pout your lips. Like this. Like you are blowing me a kiss.

She tries to copy him. He holds the brochure up and looks at her.

Now, put your hands above your head. Behind your head. That's it. Good. But, Lumi, hold your stomach in!

He sits back and looks at her. She readjusts slightly, giving a slight look of discomfort.

What?

LUMINITA. Sorry.

LEKO. What is the matter?

LUMINITA. Nothing.

LEKO. You're tired?

LUMINITA. No.

LEKO. You're tired, Luminita?

LUMINITA. Just a little bit.

LEKO. It's been a long night.

Beat. He puts down the Bell's. He looks at the brochure, and then puts it to one side.

Take your hands down.

She does with relief.

Now put your hands on your tits. And arch your back, Luminita. Jesus, I thought you wanted to be a sexy model. I thought you were going to make us rich. (*Begins to laugh.*) Aren't you going to make us rich, Luminita?

LUMINITA. Yes.

LEKO. So be sexy. BE *SEXY*!

Pause. LEKO *sighs and shakes his head.*

If you want to you can put your hand on the wall.

LUMINITA. Thank you.

LEKO. Now. Now turn around. Look over your shoulder at me.

She does. It's difficult to keep up. LEKO *lights a cigarette and lies back on the bed, blowing smoke rings.*

Luminita, are you happy?

LUMINITA. Yes.

LEKO. Are you?

LUMINITA. Yes.

Beat.

LEKO. I am not happy. You know how much trouble that bitch Mimi has caused me?

LUMINITA. No I don't.

LEKO. Ask me how much.

LUMINITA. How much, Leko?

LEKO. A fucking lot. If she wasn't dead I would kill her myself.

LUMINITA *reacts to this by dropping her position slightly.* LEKO *claps his hands. She snaps back.*

I miss my country. If we were in Albania I would have you as my wife, Lumi. We would visit my parents' house and my mother would teach you how to be a woman. You would like it there, Lumi.

But the people in my country are ugly and fucking backward. I was the first Bardici brother to leave my country, you know that? I am the youngest, Lumi. My brothers used to laugh at me when I had to stay in and help my mother prepare dinner, and when my dad used to beat me because he was drunk and I was the smallest. Who's laughing now? Hey, Luminita?

LUMINITA. Yes.

LEKO. People here are ugly too. But they are more clever. Do you know who are the ugliest people here, Lumi?

LUMINITA. No.

LEKO. The women. The English women. With their foul mouths and their cigarettes. Their guts hanging over the top of their tight tight trousers, and their binge-drinking and their bleached hair. Vomiting in the street. The English women. They make me sick, Lumi. If my wife behaved like that I would shoot her in the head. Now turn back to me. Hands on hips again.

Beat. She does. She manages to find a more comfortable compromise.

So I miss my country, a little bit. Sometimes at night I cry when I think about Albania and my mother and my father and when I was a little boy. Do you believe that? Lumi?

LUMINITA. Umm...

LEKO. Do you believe that I go to bed at night and cry for my country and the people I love? Do you?

Beat.

LUMINITA. No.

LEKO (*sharply*). Why not?

LUMINITA. Because you never go to sleep at night. You sleep in the day.

He laughs.

LEKO. That is very good, Luminita. If I was your teacher I would give you a gold star.

Beat. He takes a swig of Bell's.

Do you cry for your country?

LUMINITA (*quietly*). No.

LEKO. Ha. No one cries for Moldova! Because Moldova is a piece of shit. Right?

LUMINITA. Right.

LEKO. But you do cry sometimes. Because I hear you.

LUMINITA. But not for a long time.

LEKO. No. Not for a long time.

Beat.

LUMINITA. I'm sorry.

LEKO. It's okay, my little chicken. I get homesick too. But we are here to work. (*Singing Aloe Blacc song.*) 'I need a dollar dollar, dollar is what I need'! (*Beat.*) Luminita, my darling?

LUMINITA. Yes?

He throws the brochure at her.

LEKO. You are no model.

She leaves her pose and turns around and just stands in front of him, head down.

But it's okay. My darling, it's okay.

Beat.

LUMINITA. Leko?

LEKO. Yes?

LUMINITA. Please may I sit down?

LEKO. Okay, lazybones.

She sits, relieved, in the corner of the room, taking off her high heels and putting them neatly next to her. She hugs her knees.

Here. Eat some chicken.

He slides her a cardboard box of chicken. She opens it, looks in, looks at LEKO.

Eat it.

She eats.

Look at me, Luminita. Look how I am sweating. Like a pig. It rains all summer, and now, in September, this heat. They call this an Indian summer, Luminita.

LUMINITA. Do they?

LEKO. They do. It stinks like India too. Of shit. (*Beat.*) Guess what?

LUMINITA. What?

LEKO. I got you a present. Ask me, what is my present, Leko?

LUMINITA. What is my present, Leko?

LEKO. Here.

He takes out of his pocket a piece of cardboard with pretty girly hair clips on it and passes it to her.

LUMINITA. Thank you, Leko.

LEKO. It is for your hair.

LUMINITA. Yes. Thank you. They are very nice.

She puts a couple in.

Beat. LUMINITA *plucks up the courage to ask.*

Leko?

LEKO. Yes.

LUMINITA. Do you think I could please have some Vaseline?

LEKO. Why?

Beat.

LUMINITA. Because it is sore… When I…

LEKO. Fuck?

LUMINITA. Yes.

LEKO. Okay.

LUMINITA. Thank you.

LEKO. I will get some for you. On Saturday. Okay?

LUMINITA. Okay. (*Beat.*) What day is it today?

LEKO. Today is Wednesday.

Beat.

LUMINITA. Okay. Thank you, Leko.

Beat. He sits up, and reaches into the plastic bag.

LEKO. Ah. Why am I so good to you? It must be love. Don't look at what I'm doing, my little chicken.

LUMINITA. Okay.

He gets out an empty Coke can which has been fashioned as a crack pipe and a stash bag.

LEKO. It is a surprise for you. Don't spoil the surprise.

LUMINITA. Okay. I won't.

LUMINITA *looks away.*

LEKO. No peeking.

LUMINITA. I'm not peeking.

LEKO *takes one of the rocks and places it in the pipe ready to smoke. He stands up and walks over to* LUMINITA.

LEKO. Look at me.

She looks up. He holds the pipe out to her. She takes it in her hand, he lights the rock for her and puts his hand on the back of her head. She inhales deeply. She falls back against the wall a little with a massive rush, her legs knock and stumble a little, the movement resembling that of startled cattle being herded into a lorry. LEKO *puts his own rock in the pipe. He fires it and takes a hit. They are both fucked.*

LEKO. Luminita?

LUMINITA. Yes?

LEKO. Come here.

LUMINITA *walks towards him unsteadily.*

Take off your clothes and go down on all fours.

*She immediately starts to take her vest off. Suddenly there is
the sound of a loud industrial doorbell downstairs. She stops.*

FUCK!

He stands with some difficulty and claps at her. LUMINITA
rushes to put on her shoes, in her fucked state. LEKO *exits.*
LUMINITA *stands waiting, looking towards the door,
attempting a sexy look.*

Scene Three

HILARY *and* KATIE *lying on the sofa.* KATIE *wearing a little
kimono.* KATIE *is massaging* HILARY*'s feet. A couple of
candles. Music playing: 'All Along the Watchtower' by Jimi
Hendrix.*

KATIE. Twenty women and children. Naked. Terrified. Seeing
white people for the first time.

HILARY. Amazing.

KATIE. They were checking the dump area where space rockets
from Woomara were scheduled to crash-land. Aussie and
British governments testing rockets on Aboriginal land.

HILARY. So what happened when they found them?

KATIE. They still tested them.

HILARY. Fucking hell.

KATIE. Multi-million-dollar operation. Who's gonna let a few
Abbo's ruin it?

HILARY. That's heartbreaking.

KATIE. I knew when I saw it I had to be around them. I knew I
was going to make them my life's work.

HILARY. You saw them?

KATIE. Yeah. On YouTube.

Beat.

HILARY. You look beautiful tonight.

KATIE. So do you.

HILARY. God, I feel a hundred years old.

KATIE. Not age *again*! Let it go, baby. You're an eternal child as far as I'm concerned.

HILARY. If you say so.

KATIE. I do. (*Beat.*) You liked dinner?

HILARY. It was… extraordinary.

KATIE. Really?

HILARY. Yep. Who knew you could do that with tofu?

KATIE. I've been at it all day. I've been marinating since three.

HILARY. You didn't paint then? (*Beat.*) Kate?

KATIE. Yeah, I might start cooking more now. I'll do dinner tomorrow, okay? Leave it to me. I'll feed the workers.

HILARY. That's lovely, Katie, but do you think…

KATIE. What?

HILARY. Well, have you ever heard of clearing as you go?

KATIE. I'm a whirlwind in that kitchen, Hils. It's art, really, isn't it? I can't be thinking about cleaning up, it stops the creative flow.

HILARY. It's just it looks a bit like a bomb's gone off in there.

KATIE. And I keep telling you, you need to get a dishwasher.

HILARY (*snapping a little*). With what?

KATIE *flinches*.

Sorry, love. It's just these things cost money. (*Beat.*) Anyway, me and Hen can look after ourselves. I want you *painting*!

KATIE. Can we not talk about it now?

HILARY. Okay. Okay, love. I'm sorry.

HILARY *does a big yawn*.

God, I'm shattered.

KATIE. Baby, you need a break. You need to de-stress.

KATIE gently kisses HILARY's toes.

Is that nice?

HILARY. Yeah, lovely.

KATIE. Wanna get an early night?

HILARY. Katie, it's six o'clock!

KATIE. Okay. Wanna come in the bedroom with me so I can fuck you?

The harshness of the statement jars with HILARY and she sits up.

HILARY. Not till he's home, love. There's no way he should be this late.

She tries HENDRIX on the phone.

Straight to voicemail. Again.

KATIE. How about a quickie on the sofa?

HILARY. No! What if he comes in?

KATIE. We'll hear the door.

HILARY. I don't want to risk it.

Beat. KATIE sulks a little and draws her knees up to her chest.

He's been acting so bloody weird recently.

KATIE. He's a teenager. It's what they do.

HILARY. I think there's something wrong. It took me twenty minutes to find him when I went to pick him up the other day. He was lolloping around the staff car park and, Kate, I think he had been crying.

KATIE. It's hormones. I was a terror when I was sixteen.

HILARY. Jesus I bet you were. What if it's drugs?

KATIE. Nah his head's too screwed on for that.

HILARY. I can't believe he's all grown up. I love being a mother. I'll miss it.

KATIE. You'll always be his mum.

HILARY. But he won't need me.

KATIE. Boys, men, they always need their mums. They're pussies.

They laugh a little.

And anyway, I was thinking. Maybe we'll have a child of our own one day.

HILARY. Really?

KATIE. Yeah. We'd make great parents. I mean there's gotta be more to life than commissions and exhibitions. I want more than that. I want a family, a proper one.

HILARY *beams.*

HILARY. That's amazing, Katie.

KATIE. I know. Isn't it? I have to kiss you now.

KATIE *straddles* HILARY *and goes to kiss her. The door slams and they quickly sit up.* HENDRIX *walks through the living room, head down, chucking his open bag (which some stuff falls out of) down by the table. He is wearing a coloured sports T-shirt under his blazer. He goes straight to his room.* HILARY *and* KATIE *look at each other.*

HILARY (*shouting*). Hendrix!

No response. She gets up and turns the music off.

I'm not having this.

HILARY *goes to the doorway.*

Hendrix, get out here now!

Reluctantly he appears, hair floppier over one side of his face, very self-conscious.

SIT.

He sits at the table but looks firmly away. HILARY *softens, goes to his level.*

What the hell is going on, dude? Where is your school shirt?

Beat.

Dude. Look at me.

She leans over and moves his face towards her. She gasps.

What's happened to your eye?

KATIE *jumps up and rushes over to* HILARY*'s shoulder. Following text is rapid, overlapping sometimes.*

He's got a cut above his eye, Kate!

KATIE. *Shit!* Hennie!

HENDRIX. Please leave it, it's nothing.

HILARY. Doesn't look like nothing.

HENDRIX. Don't touch it, Mother!

HILARY. It's bleeding.

HENDRIX. OW! Fuck.

KATIE. I'll get the first-aid box.

KATIE *runs out.* HENDRIX *breathes deeply and* HILARY *rubs his back.*

HENDRIX. Please, Mum, just get off.

HILARY. Do you want a glass of water?

KATIE *runs in with the first-aid kit.*

I think he's having a panic attack.

HENDRIX. I am NOT having a panic attack, Mother. I'm fine.

Beat.

HILARY. Shall I clean it up?

HENDRIX. No.

KATIE. Shall I do it?

HENDRIX. No!

KATIE. I've got first-aid training.

HILARY. Come on, darling. It might go septic.

HENDRIX. Fine! But you do it, *not* her.

KATIE passes the first-aid kit to HILARY *and skulks to the side of the room, feeling rejected.* HILARY *cleans it up.*

Ow! Can't you be more gentle?

HILARY. Sorry! (*Looking at* KATIE.) I wonder if we should just pop down to A&E.

KATIE. It might need a stitch.

HENDRIX. It doesn't need a stitch. I'm fine!

HILARY. Okay. Okay.

She finishes. The dust settles a little.

There. You'll live. Hendrix, have you been fighting?

HENDRIX. No!

HILARY. Darling, I mean it –

HENDRIX. I haven't!

KATIE. Hennie's a lover not a fighter –

HENDRIX. Fuck off!

HILARY. This isn't funny, Katie – !

KATIE. I know! I'm sorry I don't know why I said it, it just slipped out.

HENDRIX. Whatever.

KATIE. I mean it!

HILARY. Okay.

HILARY turns to HENDRIX.

You know we think violence of any type is wrong.

KATIE gets up and starts to pick up stuff from HENDRIX's *school bag where it has spilt out.*

HENDRIX. I don't want to talk about it!

HILARY. Well, we're *going* to talk about it!

HENDRIX. Please may I go to my room?

HILARY. This is serious, Hendrix – !

HENDRIX. I'm missing *The Gadget Show*!

HILARY. Fuck *The Gadget Show*!

KATIE. What the *fuck*?

> KATIE *is holding out* HENDRIX*'s school shirt, on the back in black marker pen are the words clearly spelt out:* 'BATTY BOY'.

HILARY. What does that say?

KATIE. It says 'Batty Boy'.

HENDRIX (*going to grab the shirt from her*). Shut up!

HILARY. Sit down, Hen! Well, what the hell does 'Batty Boy' mean. Hey?

> *Beat. Nothing from* HENDRIX.

KATIE. It means gay.

HILARY. As in homosexual?

> KATIE *nods*.

Does it, Hen? (*Beat.*) Right I'm ringing the school!

HENDRIX. NO, MUM! You CAN'T!

HILARY. If you think I'm going to have my sixteen-year-old son coming home from school, with a cut eye and fucking... fucking 'batty boy' scrawled all over his shirt you've got another thing coming!

HENDRIX. Please!

KATIE. I don't think you should ring the school, Hils. There'll be no one there now anyway –

HILARY. So what the hell do you suggest I do?

KATIE. Don't shout at me!

HILARY. Right. Tomorrow morning I'm driving you in and we are going straight to the principal's office so we can tell him just what's been going on in his bloody school –

HENDRIX. MUM! They'll KILL me!

Pause. This quietens everyone. HENDRIX *is head in hands.* HILARY *is shocked.* KATIE *sees her opportunity to get involved.*

KATIE. Okay. Everyone, let's all calm down and chill out. Okay? Hils, take a seat. Hen, you've obviously had a horrible shock, babes. Do you want some Rescue Remedy?

HENDRIX. No I DON'T want any FUCKING Rescue Remedy!

KATIE. Okay. Okay.

HENDRIX (*to* HILARY). Can I have a glass of wine?

HILARY. I don't think that's appropriate right now.

HENDRIX. Oh, Mum!

KATIE. Let him have a little glass, Hils. Let's all have one. I'm shaking.

HILARY. Go on then.

KATIE *pours them all a glass.*

HENDRIX. Have we got any red?

HILARY. Don't push your luck.

They all take a sip of wine.

So?

HENDRIX. I'm just getting a bit of a hard time. That's all.

HILARY. What do you mean a 'hard time'?

HENDRIX. You know.

HILARY. Violence?

HENDRIX. Sometimes.

HILARY. This is totally unacceptable.

HENDRIX. It's not always like this. It's usually just pranks and name-calling.

HILARY. Who?

HENDRIX. Does it matter?

HILARY. Yes it absolutely matters.

HENDRIX. Just some guys in my year.

HILARY. Right.

HENDRIX. And some guys in the year above.

Beat. He downs his small glass of wine.

HILARY. Okay. How long?

HENDRIX. A couple of weeks.

HILARY. Weeks?

HENDRIX. Yeah. Since term started. Before they just ignored me. I didn't mind that.

HILARY. Names?

HENDRIX. You don't know anyone at my school so what difference would it make?

He gets up.

HILARY. Sit DOWN!

He sits. He pours himself another glass. HILARY *clocks this but chooses to ignore it.*

Why?

HENDRIX. Why what?

HILARY. Why you?

HENDRIX. Why not?

HILARY. Don't be smart, Hendrix.

HENDRIX *sighs.*

HENDRIX. God, because, Mother. *Because.*

HILARY. Because of me?

Beat. He looks at her.

HENDRIX. What do you want me to say?

HILARY *gets up and walks away for a moment, taking it in. She begins to cry. Not a regular occurrence.* HENDRIX *and* KATIE *look at each other.*

I'm sorry, Mum. Mum?

KATIE. Oh God, Hils, please don't cry!

HENDRIX. Stop it, Mum.

HILARY. I don't understand. There's zero proof that a child from a same-sex relationship is any more likely to be homosexual!

HENDRIX. I know!

HILARY. And you're not!

HENDRIX. I know!

HILARY. Are you?

HENDRIX. Am I what? Homosexual? No! God's sake, Mum!

KATIE. It's nothing to be ashamed of, Hen.

HENDRIX. I know that, but I'm not!

KATIE. All of my best friends back home are gay.

HENDRIX (*totally exasperated*). Will you both please listen to what I'm saying. I'M NOT GAY!

HILARY. Okay. Okay, Hen. It's just ridiculous that they would think that just because of me...

HENDRIX. Tell that to a class of sixteen-year-old boys.

HILARY. I suppose.

KATIE. Yeah. I suppose.

Beat.

HILARY. Hang on. I thought nobody knew. How did they find out?

Beat. HENDRIX *takes a deep breath.*

HENDRIX. In the holidays Abdul Kassir and his dad went to Ikea.

HILARY. Right?

HENDRIX. They were in the car park.

Beat.

HILARY. Oh Jesus.

HENDRIX. He said he saw you and Katie... messing around in the car.

HILARY. Oh Jesus fucking Christ.

HENDRIX (*quietly*). He said you were practically dogging.

HILARY. Oh God.

A look exchanged between KATIE *and* HILARY.

HENDRIX. We're just lucky his phone battery was dead.

HILARY. What? Oh shit a brick. Yes, thank God.

Pause. They take all this in. HILARY *gathers herself.*

Well, you know what? Fuck 'em, Hen! Fuck Them! So we're in love? So we're passionate about each other? Just because their parents probably only have sex with the lights out on a Saturday night after *Britain's Got Talent.*

HENDRIX. Well, that's better than in an Ikea car park!

KATIE. If it was a straight couple no one would care. They'd probably think it was great!

HENDRIX. I went into school the next day and someone had written 'Hendrix's Mum Munches Rug' on the board!

KATIE. Eugh!

HILARY. Please don't use that expression, Hendrix!

HENDRIX (*exasperated*). I'm just telling you what they said!

HILARY. And this has been going on since then?

HENDRIX. Pretty much. But today it's been worse. Something happened in the showers.

KATIE *and* HILARY. What???

HENDRIX. God nothing – nothing bad! It's just I was looking one way and some guy said I was looking at his... at him, when I wasn't. I was just off in my own world a bit. It must have looked that way. It's just got a bit out of hand.

Beat.

HILARY. And they hurt you?

HENDRIX *shrugs.*

Can you tell me how?

HENDRIX (*holding tears back*). I really don't want to, Mum. Can we talk about this tomorrow? Please?

HILARY. I'm sorry, Hendrix. I should have been more aware with what was going on with you. I'm sorry.

Beat.

HENDRIX (*shrugs*). Okay.

HILARY. Does this make me a bad mother?

HENDRIX. No. (*Beat.*) Can I go to my room now?

She regroups.

HILARY. Okay. Okay, champ! We'll talk about this tomorrow night, right? Put together a game plan.

KATIE. Take some positive action.

HILARY. No one is ever powerless.

HENDRIX. Right. Yeah. Got it.

HILARY. But you're going to be okay, going in tomorrow? Are you?

HENDRIX. Yeah. Fine.

HILARY. *Bon courage.*

HENDRIX (*joining in with her*). *Bon courage.* Yeah yeah I know.

He goes to his room. KATIE *puts her arm around* HILARY.

Scene Three to Four transition:

Lights fade up on LUMINITA *sitting on the end of the bed, eating from a small cardboard box of chicken. Lights fade on* HILARY *and* KATIE. *When* LUMINITA *has finished she closes the box and puts it in the waste-paper bin which is under the bed. She takes her washbag out and uses face wipes to give her hands and mouth a good wipe. There is a sense of ritual. She throws the wipes away and gets a can of Tyskie (Polish lager) out from under the bed. She cracks the can and takes a drink, then sets it down next to her. She holds her hand over her chest and is still for a moment as though she might be sick. She manages to quell the nausea and lies down on the bed with her eyes open. Lights fade.*

Scene Four

HENDRIX *lies in his bed. Radiohead 'Reckoner' plays on his modest stereo. He is under his duvet, wanking. The lights are off so he is barely visible, but the movement is clear.* KATIE *pops her head in the door.*

KATIE (*whispering*). Hen?

HENDRIX. God!

He flips over in bed and kneels up, covering himself. He is wearing boxers and a T-shirt.

What do you want? Shit!

KATIE *steps into the room, turning the light on. She is carrying two very large glasses of red wine. She is a little pissed.*

KATIE. Can I come in?

HENDRIX. Well, you're in, aren't you?

KATIE. What were you doing?

HENDRIX. Nothing!

KATIE (*smiling*). Hendrix – ?

HENDRIX. What do you want, Katie? It's one o'clock in the morning!

KATIE. I wanted to give you this.

KATIE *holds out a glass of wine.*

It's that Pinot that you like.

Beat. Suspicious, but ultimately in need of a drink, he takes it.

HENDRIX. I thought you were on white.

KATIE. We drank it all. Then Hils passed out. I couldn't sleep. I couldn't stop thinking about you.

HENDRIX. What?

KATIE. I couldn't stop thinking about you. (*Beat.*) And this bullying stuff. I wanted to give you some advice.

HENDRIX. I'm really not up for this.

KATIE. If you want to stop it happening, you need to hear this. Shift up.

Intrigued, HENDRIX *makes room for her on the end of the bed, but keeps as far away from her as possible.*

You know I was bullied at school. Big time.

HENDRIX. Because you were gay?

KATIE. Hell no. I was into guys then. Anyway, I don't like labels. I like who I like. You know?

HENDRIX. Okay.

KATIE. I had an awful bloody time. The girls hated me because I was smart and attractive but mainly because I started to develop breasts before anyone else.

HENDRIX *chokes a little on the wine.*

I used to come home covered in scratches and bite marks, with wet hair where my head had been flushed down the can.

HENDRIX. What did your mum say?

KATIE. Oh she was too bombed out of her head to notice most of the time. Anyway, this went on for weeks. I couldn't sleep, and I'd throw up every last scrap of food I ate. I started skipping class and hanging around all day at the park. But then they found me.

HENDRIX. That's horrible, Katie.

KATIE. Yup. Worst time of my life. Anyway, these girls were really into their catfighting, right? Biting and scratching and hair-pulling; no fists involved. So I put together a totally Trojan plan. I started boxing training at the local gym with this awesome ex-national boxer. Taught me to fight like a man.

HENDRIX. Shit.

KATIE. So the main girl was Kerri Winterson. One day at break she dragged me across the playground by my hair then tore off my shirt so everyone could see my tits. And something inside me snapped. It was time. I found my feet, made a fist, then with every little bit of spirit and venom I had I smashed it into her goofy fucking face. And do you know what, Hen?

HENDRIX. What?

KATIE. Not only did I break her nose, but I shattered her fucking cheekbone.

Beat.

HENDRIX. Jesus.

KATIE. And I broke her glasses.

HENDRIX. No shit.

KATIE. I identified her weakness. None of the girls ever touched me again and all the boys wanted to fuck me. That was my rite of passage. (*Beat. Drinks.*) That's what you gotta do, Hen. Identify their weakness. I bet they go for headlocks, dead arms and upper-body punches, right?

HENDRIX. Sort of, yeah.

KATIE. Then you go in low. Stomach, thighs, goolies. Join a gym. Get training. Hit them where it hurts.

HENDRIX. I'm not a fighter, Katie.

KATIE. Bullshit.

HENDRIX. I'm not. I think violence of any description is wrong.

KATIE. That sounds like Hilary talking. Who's the main guy?

HENDRIX. There's a few. But probably Jason Parsons. He's a dick. His dad votes UKIP.

KATIE. Ooh yuck. Right, well, next time Jason Parsons is on his own, stride straight up to him, grab him by the throat and give him a powerhouse punch right in the nads.

Beat. HENDRIX *considers this.*

HENDRIX. I don't know.

KATIE. Seriously. Identify his weakness. (*Nudges him playfully.*) Listen to Katie! She doesn't talk bollocks all the time.

HENDRIX *smiles a little. It is a moment of warmth between them.* HENDRIX *drinks.*

Kerry Winterson's dead now. Boob cancer.

HENDRIX. Gosh.

KATIE. Karma, babes. Your mum's very worried.

HENDRIX. I know.

KATIE. I hate to see her like that.

HENDRIX. Me too.

KATIE. I told her I didn't think you were gay.

HENDRIX. I'm not.

KATIE. I know. Do you know how I know?

Beat.

HENDRIX. How?

KATIE *leans back a little on the bed.*

KATIE. The first night I met you and your mum. The opening of my exhibition. You were chatting to me so articulately about my work I couldn't believe you were only sixteen. You know when you walked in with Hils, I thought you were a couple.

HENDRIX. Really?

KATIE. Yup. Hot forty-something with a hot twenty-something I thought.

HENDRIX. No way. Gross.

KATIE. You were knocking back the free red like a trouper and your mum was getting vexed. I thought it was so funny, and sweet. The way you were with each other. She went into the blue room, and you stayed yabbering with me and spilled wine all down your shirt. Do you remember?

HENDRIX. Sort of.

KATIE. I took you into the toilet, into this little cubicle, to sponge it down so it didn't stain, do you remember?

HENDRIX. Not really.

KATIE. We were very close. I could feel how nervous you were, how… excited.

HENDRIX. I think you might have / this wrong.

KATIE. You nearly kissed me.

Beat.

HENDRIX. No I didn't.

KATIE. Yes you did.

HENDRIX. Is that what you told my mum?

KATIE. Of course not! That's our secret, Hendrix. For always.

HENDRIX. Fuck's sake.

KATIE. Relax.

KATIE *leans back a little, puts her hand up to* HENDRIX*'s hair and begins to stroke the hair behind his ears. After a couple of seconds* HENDRIX *pulls away.*

HENDRIX. I was just swaying around. I'd come straight from school. I hadn't had any dinner.

KATIE *laughs.*

KATIE. If you say so, babes.

Beat.

HENDRIX. Is Mum okay?

KATIE. She's in bits. She loves you. (*Beat.*) You're so lucky, Hen. My mum was a total cunt to me. She used to be a reasonably successful soap actress, did you know that?

HENDRIX. No I didn't.

KATIE. Have you heard of a soap called *Sons and Lovers*?

HENDRIX. I might have.

KATIE. Well. My mum played Barbara, she was a returning character. A dog-walker.

HENDRIX. Wow.

KATIE. Then I was born and she had really bad post-natal depression. She never went back to acting, and she never forgave me. But Hils, she's an amazing mum. She's in bits right now.

HENDRIX. I'll speak to her tomorrow. Tell her not to worry.

KATIE. I'm glad we've had this chat. I have a feeling we might have got off on the wrong foot.

HENDRIX. Yeah. (*Beat.*) Thanks, Katie.

KATIE. I know I've only been here a few months, and I know that's nowhere near as long as what's-her-name.

HENDRIX (*annoyed*). Meg.

KATIE. Yeah, yeah. And I'm not trying to replace her.

HENDRIX. You couldn't.

KATIE. That's what I'm saying, Hen. Me and Meg, we're nothing alike, believe me, I've seen pictures. But we could be a family, don't you think? You could be like the little bro I never had.

Beat.

HENDRIX. I guess.

She plants a warm platonic kiss on his cheek. She jumps up, and spots her jumper hanging over the chair.

KATIE. Oh my God! My fave jumper! I've been wondering where I left it. Hold this.

She passes him her wine. Without hesitation she takes her dressing gown off and chucks it to the floor. Turned from the audience, she is topless and just wearing little shorts, and HENDRIX *can see her breasts clearly. He is open-mouthed, frozen. She holds the jumper out to look at it, and then throws the jumper on and turns to* HENDRIX. *She picks up her dressing gown.*

Thanks, babes.

She smiles and takes her wine. He leaves his hand where it was, frozen. She goes to the door, glances back.

Don't tell your mum about the Pinot. She'll go nuts. Night.

She is gone. HENDRIX *looks after her, still in the same position.*

HENDRIX. Fuck.

Lights fade on HENDRIX.

Scene Five

Lights come up on LUMINITA *on her hands and knees scrubbing away at the top of the mattress. She has a bowl of warm soapy water.* LEKO *strides into the room eating a piece of chicken.*

LEKO. That's not clean yet?

LUMINITA. It's nearly.

LEKO. I have a customer downstairs.

LUMINITA. It's nearly clean.

Beat. LEKO *paces a little.*

It's early for a customer.

LEKO. And?

LEKO *throws the chicken bone in the bin. He sniffs the air deeply.*

It fucking stinks.

LUMINITA. Shall I open the window?

LEKO. Don't be stupid. Don't open the window. Spray the spray.

LUMINITA *gets a plastic box of cleaning products out from under the bed, gets some air freshener out and wafts it in the general direction.*

Give it to me.

He sprays the mattress directly. He sniffs it.

What the fuck is this?

LUMINITA. It's lavender.

He sniffs again. Sprays again.

LEKO. Why was he sick?

LUMINITA. He was drunk.

LEKO. It wasn't something you did.

LUMINITA. No. Of course not, Leko.

LEKO. Ahh... I'm only joking, chicken! Look at you. How could you ever do something to make someone puke? But I will have to get this cleaned now.

He grabs her wrist.

Don't let it happen again.

LUMINITA. Okay. I won't.

LEKO (*relaxed again*). Now, I think you are going to like this guy, Lumi.

LUMINITA (*alarmed*). Why?

LEKO. Don't ask me why. You trust me yes?

LUMINITA. Yes.

LEKO. Good.

He kisses her on the head.

Smile, Luminita!

Still concerned, she manages a forced smile.

Jesus, Lumi. You are no fun.

He goes. She puts the cleaning products away, sniffs the mattress and quickly throws the duvet over it, straightening it. She goes and stands next to the wall and takes up one of the 'sexy' positions from before, with her hands on her hips and her lips pouting. She stays like this. She hears LEKO's laugh. LEKO enters, with HENDRIX trailing behind. HENDRIX is out of uniform, wearing jeans and a black hooded jumper. He is beyond nervous.

Here we go! This is Luminita!

LEKO presents her. LUMINITA gives a little wave.

HENDRIX. Hello.

LEKO. Give him a little spin, baby.

She does.

Come here, Lumi.

LEKO *puts his arms around them both*.

This is the best girl I have ever had.

HENDRIX *nods nervously and smiles at* LUMINITA *politely*.

HENDRIX. Okay.

LEKO. She's very beautiful. And she's very clean. What do you think?

Pause.

HENDRIX. Uh… Very nice.

LEKO (*laughing*). Very nice? Very nice! There you go, baby. What's your name, boy?

HENDRIX. Is it okay if I don't say?

LEKO. We need your name, my friend. We need them for our records.

HENDRIX. Seriously?

LEKO. Of course.

HENDRIX (*starting to back out of the room*). Look, maybe I should just…

LEKO *starts to laugh heartily*.

LEKO. Look, Lumi! Look at his face!

HENDRIX *hovers awkwardly in the doorway*.

Laugh! It's funny!

LUMINITA *starts to laugh. Eventually* HENDRIX *joins in. They laugh for a few seconds and then it starts to fade*.

It's fine. We'll just call you 'stud'. Right, Lumi?

LUMINITA. Right.

HENDRIX. No seriously, I'd like to remain anonymous if that's okay?

LEKO. I like this guy. No problem no problem. Luminita is working here to go to university. That's right isn't it, baby?

LUMINITA *nods*.

HENDRIX. Oh wow. Which uni?

LUMINITA *looks at* LEKO.

LEKO. London University.

HENDRIX. Oh, what, UCL?

LEKO *looks at* LUMINITA.

LUMINITA. Yes.

HENDRIX. It's a good place.

Beat. LEKO *looks at the cut above* HENDRIX*'s eye*.

LEKO. Been fighting, stud?

HENDRIX. Oh this? No I just... Well, actually yeah, just a little fight.

LEKO. You need to watch this one, Lumi!

HENDRIX. Oh God! No, don't worry, I would never / dream of –

LEKO. It's a joke, my friend. Loosen up!

HENDRIX. Oh. Okay.

Beat.

LEKO. You want some chicken when you're done?

HENDRIX. No thank you.

LEKO. It's good chicken.

HENDRIX. No, thank you. I'm fine.

LEKO. What are you, a fucking vegetarian?

HENDRIX. No... (*Beat.*) No some chicken would be great. Thank you.

LEKO (*businesslike all of a sudden*). Lumi, he wants 'The Girlfriend Experience' and he wants to bag up. Okay?

LUMINITA. Okay.

LEKO. Get him a drink. And be gentle with him.

LUMINITA. Okay.

He looks at HENDRIX, *grins, and slaps him hard on the back.*

LEKO. Okay?

HENDRIX. Okay.

LEKO *leaves chuckling to himself. They stand for a moment.* HENDRIX *is supremely awkward.* LUMINITA *becomes fairly monotone, as though on autopilot.*

LUMINITA. You want a drink?

HENDRIX. Yes, please.

LUMINITA. You want a beer?

HENDRIX. Yes please.

LUMINITA. You can sit down.

HENDRIX. Okay. Thanks.

She gets a Tyskie out of the crate and passes it to him. She sits down on the bed and leans back a little, taking a seductive pose but with a sense of blankness.

Thanks. Ah. Polish beer.

LUMINITA. It's okay for you?

HENDRIX (*looks at can*). Yeah yeah fine. Strong.

LUMINITA. Mmm-hmmm.

HENDRIX (*finding the percentage*). Five point six.

LUMINITA. Yes.

HENDRIX. That's stronger than Stella.

LUMINITA. Is it?

HENDRIX. Yes. Aren't you having one?

LUMINITA. No.

HENDRIX *cracks it and takes a long drink. He smiles at* LUMINITA *and looks around the room.*

HENDRIX. Gosh this room's got high ceilings.

LUMINITA. So what do you want to do, stud?

HENDRIX (*embarrassed*). You don't have to call me that.

LUMINITA. What would you like me to call you?

HENDRIX. You don't have to call me anything, do you?

    LUMINITA *shrugs*.

LUMINITA. So what do you want to do?

HENDRIX. Umm…

LUMINITA. What is it that you like?

HENDRIX. I know this is going to sound really stupid. But I don't know.

LUMINITA. You don't know?

HENDRIX. No. Sorry. I know it's silly.

LUMINITA. It's not silly. You want a massage?

HENDRIX. Oh… okay. If that's okay.

LUMINITA. That's okay. Take off your top.

    He takes his jumper off but leaves his T-shirt on.

HENDRIX. That's better. It's so hot in here. Like my house.

    She starts to massage him, quite vigorously and a little impatiently.

LUMINITA. Is that nice?

HENDRIX. Yes.

LUMINITA. You like that?

HENDRIX. Yes. I do.

LUMINITA. You are very tense.

HENDRIX. I'm a bit stressed out.

    This makes LUMINITA *laugh a little.*

    What?

LUMINITA. Nothing.

Beat.

HENDRIX. What are you going to study at uni?

LUMINITA. I don't know.

HENDRIX. Fees are really expensive, aren't they? Especially now.

LUMINITA. Yes, they are.

HENDRIX. How long will it take you, working here, to make enough money?

LUMINITA. Oh, a long long long time.

HENDRIX. That's a shame. (*Beat. Takes another sip.*) It's hot up here, Lumi– how do you say your name?

LUMINITA. Luminita.

HENDRIX. Lum-inita?

LUMINITA. LU-MI-NI-TA.

HENDRIX. Right. Yeah. It's hot up here.

LUMINITA. It's an Indian summer.

HENDRIX. It is. It feels like there's a storm about to break all the time, but it never does.

LUMINITA. Why don't you take your T-shirt off?

HENDRIX. It smells a bit funny too.

LUMINITA (*stops massaging, worried*). Like vomit?

HENDRIX. Er… yeah. Sort of.

LUMINITA. Do I smell like vomit?

HENDRIX. No, why, were you sick?

LUMINITA. No, one of the customers was sick.

HENDRIX. *On* you?

LUMINITA. On the bed. But some of it got on me.

HENDRIX. That's pretty grim.

LUMINITA (*shrugs*). Sometimes it happens.

HENDRIX. Sort of like an occupational hazard? Shit. Sorry. That sounded awful. I didn't mean that, sorry.

LUMINITA. I don't know what it meant anyway.

Beat.

HENDRIX. Why don't you open a window?

LUMINITA. I can't.

HENDRIX. Why?

LUMINITA. It's stuck.

HENDRIX. Do you want me to try?

LUMINITA. No. (*Beat.*) Would you mind not saying?

HENDRIX. Not saying what?

LUMINITA. That the room smelt of vomit?

HENDRIX. Who to? Oh to the man downstairs! God, no of course not!

LUMINITA. I wouldn't want him to think that I had spoiled your experience.

HENDRIX. Of course not. Don't be silly.

LUMINITA *laughs a little.*

What?

LUMINITA. You say 'silly' a lot.

HENDRIX. Do I?

LUMINITA. Have you been here before?

HENDRIX. Yes once. I went out in Central London with a friend and then we came here when we got off the Tube.

LUMINITA. Just two of you?

HENDRIX. Yes.

LUMINITA. Who did you see?

HENDRIX. Sorry?

LUMINITA. Who did you see? It wasn't me. Was it?

HENDRIX. Oh God – sorry! I thought you meant the chicken shop downstairs! *Roosters!* We came for fried chicken after we'd been out.

LUMINITA. What is *Roosters*?

HENDRIX. It's… the name of the shop. The name of the shop below. You must know that, surely!

LUMINITA. Ah yes, I had just forgotten.

HENDRIX. I've never been up here. Sorry. I feel silly now.

LUMINITA. Silly again?

HENDRIX. What? Oh, yes. (*Beat.*) How many people work here?

LUMINITA. Just me, at the moment. There was another girl. But she went away. I'm very busy, all the time.

HENDRIX. Oh I see. (*Beat.*) Have you tried the chicken downstairs?

LUMINITA. It's all I eat.

HENDRIX. Seriously?

She nods.

That's not a very balanced diet.

LUMINITA. No shit. Do you have a girlfriend, stud?

HENDRIX. No. Not right now.

LUMINITA. How did you know we were here?

HENDRIX. It was in the back of the *Informer*.

LUMINITA. What's that?

HENDRIX. Local paper.

LUMINITA. Oh. Was there a story about it?

HENDRIX. No. An ad.

He turns to LUMINITA, *she stops for a moment.*

I wouldn't normally dream of doing something like this.

LUMINITA. 'Something like this'?

HENDRIX. Yes. I expect everyone says that, don't they?

LUMINITA. No. They don't.

HENDRIX. Oh. Well, maybe I should explain that –

LUMINITA (*sharply*). No don't tell me.

HENDRIX. Okay.

LUMINITA *goes round and sits on his lap. She takes his beer and puts it on the ground. She is quite matter-of-fact and a little detached.*

LUMINITA. What do you want to do now?

HENDRIX. Ummm.

LUMINITA. What do you want to do? You can do whatever you want to me.

HENDRIX. Um… Could I kiss you?

LUMINITA. Yes you can kiss me.

HENDRIX. Is that okay?

LUMINITA. You can do whatever you want to me.

HENDRIX. Oh. Okay.

He goes in awkwardly, eyes closed and kisses her.

Umm… do you think you could close your eyes?

She does. He kisses her again.

Do I taste of beer?

LUMINITA. Give me your hand.

She takes his hand and guides it up her top, resting it on one of her breasts.

Go on. You can squeeze it. Don't be scared.

He does.

Does it feel nice?

HENDRIX. Errr.... Yes.

LUMINITA. Do you like it?

HENDRIX. I – I can't fucking do this!

He takes his hand away and jumps up, she slips off his lap and she knocks the can of beer over.

Oh my God I'm so sorry!

LUMINITA. It's okay.

HENDRIX. Seriously – this isn't me. I think I'm just really out of my depth here!

LUMINITA. Relax! I need to get a cloth.

HENDRIX. I'm just mega *mega* nervous. I'm sorry.

LUMINITA. Forget it. I just need to clean this up so it doesn't smell.

She goes to the bed and pulls out the box of cleaning stuff. She cleans up the beer. She is frantic, worried about it staining or smelling. HENDRIX *paces.*

HENDRIX. Can I help you with that?

LUMINITA. No.

Thank you.

HENDRIX (*to himself*). Smooth, Hendrix. Real smooth. You're such a fucking loser.

LUMINITA (*looking up for a moment*). Your name is Hendrix?

HENDRIX. Yeah.

LUMINITA. That's a funny name.

HENDRIX. Yep. My mum's got a killer sense of humour.

She sniffs the carpet. She takes the cleaning stuff back and places it neatly in the crate. He watches her. She takes a plastic Tupperware from under the bed, she takes her knickers off, places them in it and then takes a condom out of it. She puts the box back.

LUMINITA. Come on, Hendrix. (*Passes him the condom.*) This end doesn't smell so bad.

She moves the pillow to the other end of the bed. She lies down and opens her legs.

Come on.

He looks between her legs, then at the condom, then back at her. There is an unfathomably awkward pause.

HENDRIX. God! It's so fucking HOT!

He starts to pull at the neck of his T-shirt. She sits up, alarmed.

LUMINITA. You're not going to be sick are you?

HENDRIX. No! It's just – God this has GOT to open.

He pulls the curtains open and afternoon sunshine floods the room. He pulls at the sash window and it flies up with ease. LUMINITA *jumps up and runs over to the door.*

LUMINITA. What are you doing?

HENDRIX. See? It's not stuck! You need some air up here. It's so fucking hot!

HENDRIX *leans out and takes a deep breath.*

LUMINITA. Please! I'm not allowed!

HENDRIX (*coming in*). Everyone needs air, Luminita.

LUMINITA. I know. I know… but…

Pause. With light and air pouring in the room is transformed. HENDRIX *sits on the chair.* LUMINITA *walks slowly towards the window. She glances behind her at the door. Kneeling on the mattress she leans out a tiny bit. She enjoys the sun on her face for a moment. She looks at* HENDRIX.

What are you doing?

HENDRIX. Putting my head between my legs.

LUMINITA. Why?

HENDRIX. Because I feel a little bit faint.

LUMINITA goes back to looking out of the window. HENDRIX drains the last of the can. LUMINITA puts her hand out of the window, palm up.

LUMINITA. Warm.

She tentatively leans a little further out. She breathes in deeply.

HENDRIX. What can you smell?

LUMINITA. Chicken. Cigarettes. (*Breathes.*) Sunshine. Shit.

HENDRIX. Sunshine doesn't smell.

LUMINITA. I know. I'm being silly. What does that say?

He walks over and looks out of the window.

HENDRIX. 'Hounslow East Station.'

LUMINITA. I see that. There!

HENDRIX. Oh. It says 'Halal Butchers'. And then underneath it says 'Chicken, Beef, Lamb'. Actually it says 'Chicken Bef Lamb'. They've missed out an 'e'. You really can't read that?

LUMINITA. I can read it a little bit.

HENDRIX. You need glasses.

LUMINITA. I think so. I get headaches.

HENDRIX. You should get them tested. Why aren't you allowed to have the window open?

LUMINITA. I'm just not.

HENDRIX. You look like you haven't seen the sun for a long time.

LUMINITA. I haven't.

HENDRIX. Why?

LUMINITA. I work from six till six. Then I sleep. Then I clean. Then I work again.

HENDRIX. Wow. You work? I mean, when you say 'work' you mean…

LUMINITA. Yes. Fuck.

HENDRIX. Shiiit. (*Beat.*) You need to take a break. Why don't you go out somewhere?

LUMINITA. For me it is only Work. Sleep. Clean. Work. Sleep. Clean.

HENDRIX. That sounds grim. You must really wanna go to uni.

She laughs a little. Beat.

LUMINITA. Why are you called Hendrix?

HENDRIX. Oh my mum's a massive fan. Jimi Hendrix. She loves all that sixties hippy shit.

LUMINITA. She sounds very cool!

HENDRIX. She's alright. Thing is, she could have called me Mitchell, after Joni Mitchell. She could have called me Dylan, after Bob Dylan. That would have been cool. She could even have called me Jimi. But Hendrix? I sound like a prize prick!

LUMINITA (*smiling*). 'Like a prize prick.'

HENDRIX. Yeah.

LUMINITA. It's unusual.

HENDRIX. I suppose. Yours is unusual too. Why are you called Luminita?

She shrugs.

Do you know what it means?

LUMINITA. It means 'Little Light'.

HENDRIX. Ahhh. (*Beat.*) Listen, I feel really stupid about all this.

LUMINITA. Don't worry about it. (*Beat.*) What does your mother do?

HENDRIX. She runs an organic-food shop.

LUMINITA. And your father?

Beat.

HENDRIX. He doesn't live with us any more. He left a couple of years ago. He's biking across Vietnam right now.

LUMINITA. On a bicycle?

HENDRIX. No. (*Smiles.*) A motorbike. He sends me postcards. Sometimes.

LUMINITA (*looking out*). Look!

HENDRIX. The plane?

LUMINITA. It's so low!

HENDRIX. Yeah. It's pretty low. We're only a couple of miles from the airport.

LUMINITA. Which airport?

HENDRIX (*laughing*). Heathrow!

LUMINITA. Oh yes. I forgot...

She looks out the window again.

Quick! Get down!

HENDRIX. What?

LUMINITA. The chicken man. Leko's cousin. I think he can see us in a reflection.

HENDRIX. He can't!

LUMINITA. In case.

HENDRIX. I don't understand why you have to hide. (*Beat.*) Oh, I get it. You're illegal, right?

LUMINITA *looks at him.*

It's okay. We had some people like you living near us once. My mum helped them out... Oh God. Sorry. 'People like you.' I'm sorry. You must think I'm –

LUMINITA. A prize prick?

HENDRIX. Yeah.

She shrugs again and lies down in the sunlight that is spilling onto the mattress.

What are you doing?

LUMINITA. Sunbathing.

HENDRIX *moves down the bed a little, and rests against the wall. Suddenly* LUMINITA *has an idea.*

May I ask you something?

HENDRIX. Sure.

LUMINITA. Do you have a phone?

HENDRIX. Yeah.

She sits up.

LUMINITA. Really?

HENDRIX. Of course!

She glances towards the door.

LUMINITA. Please may I use it? Just for one minute?

HENDRIX. I would but / it's –

LUMINITA. Please?

HENDRIX. It's got no battery. See?

He gets his phone out of his pocket.

I let it run out on purpose because my mum keeps calling me and when I get in I say to her 'Look, Mum, no battery. See?' I'm sorry.

LUMINITA. It's okay.

Beat. LUMINITA *is crestfallen.*

HENDRIX. This has been a funny day.

LUMINITA *has an idea. She jumps up. She closes the window, trying to stay as out of sight as possible. She closes the curtains. The room is plunged into gloom.*

LUMINITA. Come here. Turn around.

He does. She gets behind him and pulls his T-shirt off. He grabs at it a little, and then lets go. He covers his chest a little, self-conscious. She starts to massage him again with a renewed, businesslike energy.

Hendrix. You are a virgin, yes?

HENDRIX (*hesitates a little*). Yes.

LUMINITA. And you don't want to be, yes?

HENDRIX. Yes. I mean no, I don't want to be.

LUMINITA. So – we will take it slow. Today we have a massage. Come back soon, and we will have a little more. Okay?

HENDRIX. Okay.

LUMINITA. We can take it nice and slow. Nice and Slow.

HENDRIX. That would be great.

LUMINITA. You just tell him you want the same. Alright? Leko. Tell him you want –

HENDRIX. 'The Girlfriend Experience.'

LUMINITA. Yes. Tell him that.

She stops massaging for a second, and runs her hands over his chest, over his nipples and kisses his shoulder lightly. He shudders. It is the most intimate he has ever been with a woman.

And you will bring a phone, with a battery. Yes?

HENDRIX. Yes. I will.

LUMINITA. Okay, Hendrix.

She continues with the massage. Lights fade up on KATIE and HILARY. HILARY is on the sofa, with a glass of wine – KATIE standing in front of her. Both couples visible. Opening bars of 'Foxy Lady' by Jimi Hendrix. The tune kicks in and KATIE dances for HILARY, wearing a vintage baby-doll nightie. LUMINITA continues to massage. Lights fade on both.

End of Act One.

ACT TWO

Scene One

HENDRIX *is lying in bed watching TV. There is a knock on the door. Assuming it to be* KATIE, *he ignores it. There is another knock. He puts the TV on mute. Sighs.*

HENDRIX. Yes?

HILARY *pops her head round the door.*

HILARY. Can I come in, Hen?

HILARY *comes in with two glasses of red wine.* HENDRIX *clicks the telly off.*

HENDRIX. What's this?

HILARY. It's that Pinot you like. I thought I had two bottles. Christ knows. I'm drinking too much.

HENDRIX. Stress.

HILARY. Yep. Here.

He takes it. He has a swig, gets up out of bed and sits on the edge. HILARY *wanders round, a bit like in an art gallery.*

I haven't been in here for a while. You've made it very individual.

HENDRIX. What's up, Mum?

HILARY. How's school? We haven't spoken about it this week. I haven't known what to say to you. I'm a very weak person sometimes.

HENDRIX. No you're not.

HILARY. I am.

HENDRIX. You're fine! I'm fine! It's all fine.

HILARY. You're chatting to people then?

HENDRIX. Well, no. But they're not beating me up. So that's a step forward.

HILARY. Have I ever told you that I'm very proud of you?

HENDRIX. Might have. Not sure.

HILARY. Well, I'm very proud of you.

HENDRIX. Thanks.

HILARY. Hendrix, I want to talk to you about pornography.

HENDRIX *chokes on his wine*.

God are you alright?

HENDRIX. You want to talk about *what*?

HILARY. I know what you've been looking at on the internet.

Beat.

HENDRIX. *How* do you?

HILARY. You left a window open.

HENDRIX. How do you know it wasn't Katie?

HILARY. Come on, Hendrix. And anyway, why would Katie be looking at straight porn?

HENDRIX. She'd look at anything, Mother. Gay, straight, dogs, horses… pigs!

HILARY. HENDRIX!

HENDRIX. I'm just saying. Why do you assume it was me?

HILARY. It was Katie that found it.

HENDRIX. Seriously?

HILARY. Yes.

HENDRIX. And she told you?

HILARY. Yes.

HENDRIX (*under his breath*). Bitch.

HILARY. WHAT?

HENDRIX. Nothing.

Beat.

HILARY. I have to say I'm surprised at what you've been –

HENDRIX. Mum, I'm really not up for discussing this –

HILARY. Well, shocked is more the word –

HENDRIX. Oh GOD –

HILARY. Or – devastated actually.

HENDRIX. Mum, I'll go vegan. I'll go gluten-fucking-free just please let's never talk about this again!

HILARY. I'm not angry – I understand that sex is a part of life –

HENDRIX. Please, Mum –

HILARY. I'm just surprised that that sort of thing would… turn you on!

HENDRIX *throws the duvet over his head.*

HENDRIX. GODDDDDD! (*From under the duvet.*) THIS is a nightmare of EPIC PROPORTIONS!

HILARY *pulls the duvet off him.*

HILARY. What is it about that sort of thing that you find arousing, Hendrix?

HENDRIX *gets up and starts pacing the room.*

HENDRIX. Arrrgh! This is a *dream.* This is *all* a *horrible* dream.

HILARY. So let's have a frank and open discussion about pornography.

HENDRIX. NO! Let's not!

HILARY. Why?

HENDRIX. Because you're my mother!

HILARY. Exactly. I'm responsible for you.

HENDRIX. Meg wouldn't have made me talk about it. Meg would have understood.

HILARY. That's not fair!

HENDRIX. Mother, you have no idea what my world is like! Whatever you saw I guarantee you there's ten times worse going round class every day on people's iPhones!

HILARY. Really?

HENDRIX. Yeah! I bet it was just run of the mill really, whatever it was.

HILARY. Run of the mill?

HENDRIX. Yeah.

HILARY. Anal sex?

HENDRIX. WHAT??

HILARY. 'Deep throating'?

HENDRIX. I can't hear you. I can't hear you. La la la la la –

    HENDRIX *immediately puts his hands over his ears.*

HILARY. The girl in that video was being totally objectified. By two men – !

HENDRIX. Mother, *please* shut UP!

    He gets back under the duvet. Beat.

HILARY. Okay. Okay. You win. God, what's *happened* to you? Where's my Hendrix who would sit up and talk to me for hours about the world and where he was going to travel and who he was going to be?

HENDRIX (*coming out from duvet*). I'm becoming a man, Mother! Or at least I'm trying to! But I keep getting – getting squashed!

HILARY. Squashed?

HENDRIX. Yes! Squashed!

HILARY. Hendrix, no one is against you! We support you – !

HENDRIX. We?

HILARY. Yes we support you in everything that you do – !

HENDRIX. WE?

HILARY. Yes. Me and Katie!

HENDRIX. Bollocks.

HILARY. Hen! (*Beat.*) Okay, so watching that sort of hard...
hard-core action – that's part of becoming a man, is it?

HENDRIX. Maybe! I don't know. I've never become a man
before. I've never *known* anyone that's become a man
before. I don't have any men in my life!

HILARY. And you've turned out okay.

HENDRIX (*not listening*). And yet – you send me to an all-
boys school! Why Hounslow Town? Why not Tafford Hall?
At least there I would have stood a chance.

HILARY. There's nothing wrong with state education. You can't
be a changer if you don't see the real world.

HENDRIX. Maybe I don't want to be a changer, Mum.

HILARY. I didn't want you to have a sense of entitlement.

HENDRIX. But they eat me for breakfast, Mother. Every day
fucking day.

Beat.

HILARY. Hendrix, I only want the best for you. Everything I've
ever done for you has been out of love. And you've not got
long left, not really.

Beat. HENDRIX *lies down on the bed, exhausted from their
exchange.*

HENDRIX. I miss Meg.

HILARY. I know you do.

HENDRIX (*sits up*) Do *you*?

Beat.

HILARY. No.

HENDRIX. Why??

HILARY. Because I've got a new life now.

HENDRIX *snorts*.

It's hard to understand I know –

HENDRIX. It's not hard to understand, Mum. It's just shit.

Beat.

HILARY. It's been a long time since she's sent you a postcard, isn't it?

HENDRIX. Yup.

HILARY. No email?

HENDRIX. Nope. I don't even know if she's still in Vietnam!

HILARY. She'll be back in touch with you when she's ready.

HENDRIX. But what about me? What if I need her?

HILARY. Let's do something together this weekend. Coffee on the South Bank and the BFI? We haven't done that for ages.

HENDRIX. Yeah cos you're too busy dogging with Katie.

HILARY. Hendrix!

HENDRIX. Meg took me out on the bike, she played tennis with me, she talked to me about things I was interested in! She gave me... confidence. She trusted me.

HILARY. I trust you.

HENDRIX. Not like she did.

HILARY. Give me an example.

HENDRIX. Okay. She let me ride the bike! She did. When I was thirteen, fourteen, twelve even! *On my own!* We did it on the wasteland near Hounslow Heath in secret because she knew you'd go mad. But she knew I could do it! She knew I'd be safe!

Beat. HILARY *is aghast.*

HILARY. Well, if that's the truth then I'm glad she's gone.

HENDRIX. FUCK OFF!

HENDRIX *turns his back to* HILARY – *a proper strop.*
Beat.

HILARY (*softly*). Hennie. It was Meg that left.

HENDRIX. You told her you didn't love her any more!

HILARY. You heard that?

HENDRIX. I hear everything in this house, Mother! You broke
her fucking heart!

HILARY. She lost interest in me! Do you understand? She *lost
interest*. I don't want to grow old gracefully, Hendrix. I want
to live. I want life.

HENDRIX. Yeah? You're alive aren't you?

HILARY. I mean I want passion. I need passion.

HENDRIX. We were a family, Mum.

HILARY. And we can be again!

HENDRIX. I hate Kate.

HILARY. You don't mean that.

HENDRIX. I do! She's like a child.

HILARY. Hey! Compassion. Empathy. Katie has her ups and
downs. At the moment she's got trouble with her creative
juices.

HENDRIX. Hasn't she just?

HILARY. We need to support her. It's traumatic for her.

HILARY. It's traumatic for me!

HILARY. You were so impressed with her at the exhibition.
Couldn't stop talking about her afterwards.

HENDRIX. I said she was nice to talk to. I didn't say move
her in.

HILARY. She's practically a celebrity, in the art world. In New
York and Sydney.

HENDRIX. I couldn't give a shit.

HILARY. Hendrix!

HENDRIX. Mother. She says 'amaze-balls'!

HILARY. Now you're just being childish.

HENDRIX. Whatever.

Pause. HILARY *sits down next to him on the bed.*

HILARY. Katie is my lover and she is my best friend.

HENDRIX. I thought I was your best friend?

HILARY. You are. You both are.

HENDRIX. Mum. Having her here. It makes me feel…
uncomfortable.

HILARY. In what way?

HENDRIX. She does things that make me feel… I don't know.

HILARY. You're being cryptic. What do you mean?

Beat. He gives up.

HENDRIX. It's just that she does things so different than Meg.
It makes me feel uncomfortable. And sad.

HILARY. Hendrix, I'm not sure if you know this, but Katie is a
very damaged person. Her life has been chaotic. She's lived
in five different countries! She's not as lucky as you and me.
Everyone deserves a chance to live a safe and happy life.
And, to be honest, she gives me things that Meg never did –

HENDRIX. What like five orgasms a night?

HILARY. Hen, that is inappropriate!

HENDRIX. You're telling me!

HILARY. I mean it is inappropriate for you to say that to me!

HENDRIX. Oh who gives a shit! Why don't you just be honest?

HILARY. Okay – I love her because she makes me feel young!
(*Beat.*) And not in the way you think. Not in a clichéd way.
In a… deep-rooted, universal way.

HENDRIX (*laughing*). Jesus!

HILARY. What?

HENDRIX. Sometimes, Mother, you talk the most unbelievable shit. (*Pause*.) Sorry.

HILARY. Oh, Hen. I wish you remembered Natasha. She was...

She glances towards the door – almost whispering.

The love of my life. When she died I would have gone under. Given up. If it hadn't been for you. You needed me. You needed to be fed, looked after, comforted. Our Hendrix became my Hendrix.

HENDRIX. I'm sorry I don't remember her.

HILARY. Then Meg came into our lives, and we were happy, for a while, weren't we?

HENDRIX. I was happy for the whole seven years, Mother.

HILARY. And then she left. I fell apart again. And it was you, again, that saved me. But this time you were doing the feeding, the comforting. I can't count the number of times you picked me up off the kitchen floor, sobbing, and put me to bed. Can you?

HENDRIX. No.

HILARY. You're a wonderful wonderful kid, Hen. But in two years' time... (*Begins to get tearful*.) You'll be gone.

HENDRIX. Who said?

HILARY. Come on. You'll be at uni. Or off on your gap year, shagging your way around Europe.

HENDRIX. Chance would be a fine thing.

She laughs at this through tears. They both do. A release.

Mum, I never said I was going to do any of that. I might just want to hang around here for a bit. Work in a pub. Get a tattoo.

HILARY. Not you, Hendrix. (*Beat*.) I don't want to be alone.

Beat. The panic sets in a little bit for HILARY *here. He sees this and puts his hand over hers.*

HENDRIX. You'll have me.

HILARY. You won't be *here* though.

HENDRIX. Not for ever. No. But…

HENDRIX *sees* HILARY*'s truth, perhaps for the first time. She breaks a little more…*

Oh… Mum.

HILARY *gets up, rubs her face, back to business.*

HILARY. It's fine. I'm fine, love. I'm sorry. God, look at me.

HENDRIX. You can talk to me.

HILARY. There's nothing to talk about. I'm being a drama queen. Silly. Look, I want you to make me a promise. Okay?

HENDRIX. Okay, sure. What?

HILARY. No more pornography. Okay?

Beat.

HENDRIX. Okay.

HILARY *kisses him on the head and gets up to leave.*

Mum, do you think maybe I could go to another school?

Beat.

HILARY. Oh, Hen. You've just got till the end of your A levels. I can't afford to send you to a private school, and any other school round here will be just like Hounslow Town.

HENDRIX. I never fit in anywhere I go.

HILARY. You fit in with me. Believe me, I want you to try and stick it out. Believe me, if you get through this period of… horrible stuff then you'll be so much a stronger person. They'll see the error of their ways. And they'll be sorry. *Bon courage?*

Beat.

HENDRIX. *Bon courage.*

HILARY. Great.

HENDRIX. Mum – Barcelona money tomorrow, yeah?

HILARY. Yep. Don't go spending it on fast cars and loose women.

HENDRIX. Hilarious, Mother.

HILARY *spots an empty chicken box. She picks it up.*

HILARY. What's this…?

She realises what it is. He is tense with disappointing her. She decides to say nothing; a small acceptance of him. She puts the box down.

Goodnight, champ.

Lights fade.

Scene Two

HENDRIX *is sitting on the bed.* LUMINITA *is kneeling behind him giving him a head massage. He has headphones hanging out of the top of his T-shirt.*

LUMINITA. What's on your earphones?

HENDRIX. Oh, I was listening to a band called Foals. Have you heard of them?

LUMINITA. Folds?

HENDRIX. FOALS – as in baby horses.

LUMINITA. Oh. No.

HENDRIX. They're my favourite band at the moment. Fucking brilliant. Do you want to have a listen?

LUMINITA. Okay.

She kneels next to him. He gets his MP3-player out and passes her the earphones to put in her ears.

HENDRIX. This one is called 'Blue Blood'.

He plays it. There is a silence. He watches her listening.

Oh actually, it takes ages before the tune kicks in, let me forward it a little bit.

He takes an earphone and listens, meaning they have to be close. He finds the bit on the track where the tune drops. He gives it back to her. She listens for eight or ten seconds. Awkward.

She passes it back.

LUMINITA. What is it about?

He takes it back and puts it back in his pocket.

HENDRIX. Umm... I'm not sure. Well, I think it's about coming home after a long time.

LUMINITA. Oh. It's very nice.

HENDRIX (*not sure whether to go on, but then deciding to*). What I like about them is that they don't just use guitars like other bands; they have brass instruments too, like trombones and trumpets. It makes me think of... I don't know. Fanfares. Of celebration. Carnival.

LUMINITA. You know a lot about music.

She goes back to massaging.

HENDRIX. I just know what I like. I like Radiohead too. What do you listen to?

LUMINITA. Oh, anything...

HENDRIX. How old are you, Luminita? Or is that rude to ask?

LUMINITA. No it's not rude. How old do you think I am?

HENDRIX. Ummmmmm, Twenty-seven? Twenty-eight?

She stops massaging.

What?

LUMINITA. I'm twenty-four.

HENDRIX (*turns around*). Shit. Sorry. I'm rubbish at things like that.

She turns him around and continues massaging.

When are you twenty-five?

LUMINITA. Soon.

HENDRIX. When?

LUMINITA. What is the date?

HENDRIX. Umm… September twenty-ninth.

Beat.

LUMINITA. Today.

HENDRIX (*turning around*). It's your birthday today?

LUMINITA. Yes.

HENDRIX. No shit!

LUMINITA. Yes.

HENDRIX. Happy birthday!

LUMINITA. Thank you.

Beat.

HENDRIX. Wow.

LUMINITA. Can I try again please?

HENDRIX. What? Oh. Yes.

He gets his phone out of his jacket which is on the bed, and gives it to her. She dials the number and listens.

LUMINITA. Where are they?

She waits a little longer. She hangs up and gives the phone back.

HENDRIX. No voicemail?

LUMINITA *shakes her head. He puts his phone back in his jacket pocket.*

Oh. I nearly forgot.

He reaches into his other jacket pocket and pulls out an apple. He passes it to LUMINITA.

Here.

LUMINITA. What's this?

HENDRIX. And… (*Also pulls out an orange*.) Here.

LUMINITA. This is for me?

HENDRIX. Yes. Oh – happy birthday!

Beat.

LUMINITA. Thank you.

HENDRIX. No problem. I thought it sounded like you weren't getting your five a day.

LUMINITA. Five what?

HENDRIX. Fruit and veg.

LUMINITA. Oh, yes.

She looks at them both for a moment, one in each hand. She doesn't know what to do with them.

Do you mind if I…

HENDRIX. Sure. Go ahead.

She chooses the apple, and puts the orange underneath her bed. She starts to eat the apple.

Can I open the window?

LUMINITA (*shakes her head*). No. (*Beat.*) This is a really nice apple.

HENDRIX. It's organic. The orange isn't though.

LUMINITA. Mmm.

HENDRIX. It'll be nice if you get to speak to your family on your birthday.

LUMINITA. Mmm.

HENDRIX. Do you miss them?

LUMINITA. I miss my sister most. Claudia.

HENDRIX. How old is she?

LUMINITA. Nine.

HENDRIX. Ah. How long since you've seen them?

LUMINITA *shrugs*.

LUMINITA. You miss your father?

HENDRIX. Yeah. Yeah I miss… Dad. Haven't heard from him in a while. He used to send postcards, emails. It was just nice having someone to talk to, when he was here. We used to talk about motorbikes and music and films. You know, man stuff.

LUMINITA. Yes.

HENDRIX. If he was here now he would know what to say about – about this trouble I'm getting at school. I mean it's nothing too bad, you know. But I think it would be good to talk to him about it.

LUMINITA. You are being bullied?

HENDRIX. No, not bullied exactly. Well, actually, yeah. (*Beat*.) I mean it's nothing I can't handle. But Mum wants to speak to the school. Mum just doesn't have a clue. She… Dad would have known what to say. Dad was good at things like that.

LUMINITA *nods and smiles*.

We don't talk about him very much in the house now. They don't like it.

LUMINITA. Who's they?

HENDRIX. My mum and – and Katie.

LUMINITA. Katie is your sister?

HENDRIX. Sort of.

LUMINITA. Sort of?

HENDRIX. Yes. She's my sister. You like the apple?

LUMINITA. It's the nicest thing I've eaten in months. Why are you being bullied?

HENDRIX. Just stuff.

LUMINITA. You seem like a really nice boy.

Beat.

HENDRIX. Thanks.

LUMINITA. I don't suppose that matters.

HENDRIX *shakes his head. Beat.*

HENDRIX. They think I'm gay.

LUMINITA. Why?

HENDRIX (*shrugs*). Cos I'm a little bit different I guess.

LUMINITA. Are you gay?

HENDRIX. NO! What do you think I'm doing here?

LUMINITA. I don't know.

HENDRIX (*sighs*). I know I'm not. I never think about men. I think about girls. I think about girls all the time!

LUMINITA *laughs a little.*

But, I don't know any girls. And I feel like if I... do it, then that'll prove for certain that I'm not. Oh – but I'm not going to tell anyone! That's not what this is about. But I'll know. That's part of it, anyway.

LUMINITA. And the other part?

HENDRIX. Umm... I really want to have sex.

LUMINITA. It was quite brave, coming here.

HENDRIX. Come on, Luminita. Thank you for saying so. But I'm a disgrace.

LUMINITA (*shrugs*). Still brave.

Beat.

HENDRIX. A group of boys in my history group went to Amsterdam at Easter. And they were saying about how they all slept with... prostitutes. And they said it was just the done thing over there. They hooked up with this stag party, and they showed them the ropes, I guess. Three of them went into this brothel and got 'the full works' while the others were queuing for a kebab.

LUMINITA. I see.

She finishes the apple and puts the core in the bin that is under the bed. She touches him on the shoulder.

Can I try again?

HENDRIX. Sure.

He takes the phone out of his pocket and gives it to her. She gets up and dials, pacing a little. HENDRIX *flops back on to the bed.*

You got rid of the smell then?

LUMINITA. Mmm.

HENDRIX (*spreading his arms out*). I feel relaxed here.

LUMINITA (*on the phone, agitated*). Come on! (*Beat.*) Shit!

She throws the phone back on the bed, exasperated. She sits on the edge of his bed. He rests up on his elbows.

HENDRIX. Still no one there? I'm sorry.

She thinks for a moment. She sits nearer to HENDRIX *and he sits up. She takes his T-shirt off, and her vest, she is wearing a bra.*

HENDRIX. What are you doing?

LUMINITA. Do you think you are ready to touch me yet, Hendrix?

HENDRIX. I don't know... Where?

LUMINITA. Here.

She takes his hand and puts it on her breast. She moves his hand around slowly.

That's good.

HENDRIX. Good.

LUMINITA (*moves his hand down and moves it up her denim skirt*). What about here?

HENDRIX *takes his hand away.*

HENDRIX. No. No I don't think I'm ready for that yet.

LUMINITA. Okay, well how about I touch you?

HENDRIX. Er... how do you mean?

LUMINITA. I can wank you if you like.

He looks totally perplexed.

You know what that is, right?

HENDRIX. Oh yeah. Believe me, I know what wanking is.

LUMINITA. Would you like that?

HENDRIX. I would. I think. I'm just nervous.

LUMINITA. Shh, lie back. Relax.

He does. She strokes his chest.

Tell me what you think about when you are wanking.

HENDRIX (*laughs*). I can't do that!

LUMINITA. Why not?

HENDRIX. I don't know. God. It's all a big mess. (*Takes a deep breath.*) Okay. I think about lots of things. Like, there's not always one thing. Lots of like images and snatches of things. Do you know what I mean?

LUMINITA. Go on.

HENDRIX. I think about stuff I've watched online, like – like the moment when… God, God I can't do this!

He sits up a little.

LUMINITA. It's okay, go on…

HENDRIX. Okay. (*Lies back. Takes a deep breath.*) Like the moment that a man enters a woman. When he actually puts his dick into her. I think about that. Or like, when she's sucking it and he cums and she swallows it. Can I really say this?

LUMINITA. Yes. It's okay.

HENDRIX. There's always loads in my head. I think about this mixed-race girl who works in PC World, she's got really nice tits and a really nice face. I think about what it would be like if – if she sucked me off and what her face would look like when I came and she swallowed it – and then – then sometimes I think about what it would look like if I came on her face. Is that bad?

LUMINITA. No, it's good.

HENDRIX. Sometimes I imagine I'm in Spearmint Rhinos or somewhere like that. (There's one in Staines.) And there's a girl like dancing in front of me, on a table, and she's bending right over and showing me her arse and her...

LUMINITA. Her pussy?

HENDRIX. Yeah and even though you're not supposed to touch them she says it's okay and I touch it and rub it and stuff. She lets me put my fingers inside her.

LUMINITA. And you like doing that?

HENDRIX. Yeah.

LUMINITA. Okay. Good, Hendrix...

She moves her hand to his crotch area and starts to rub it. He clocks what she is doing and becomes more aroused and yet more uncomfortable.

HENDRIX. But then, when I'm getting closer and I'm gonna – I'm gonna cum, it's like it all goes into overdrive. I see the girl from PC World but I'm grabbing the back of her head and I'm making her suck it or I hold the Spearmint Rhino girl down while I shove my dick in her, and I grab her tits and – and it's not nice! It's wrong! But it makes me want to cum even more!

LUMINITA. It's okay –

HENDRIX. It's not you can't treat people like that – !

LUMINITA. Life is different than sex, Hendrix.

HENDRIX. I guess....

LUMINITA. Do you feel horny now?

HENDRIX. I guess.

LUMINITA. Okay.

She unbuttons his flies and is just about to get his cock out when he jumps up.

HENDRIX. Sorry.

He turns away. He adjusts his trousers and does them up.

Can I have a beer please?

She gets a Tyskie out from under the bed and passes it to him. He cracks it and drinks. He paces a little.

Why don't you try your family again?

LUMINITA. Okay.

He points to where the phone is. She picks it up. HENDRIX *takes a large swig.*

HENDRIX. I just don't think I can do it if you're not enjoying it.

LUMINITA *is not listening.*

LUMINITA (*quietly, barely containing her excitement*). CLAUDIA??!

Throughout the conversation she is conscious of the door, and looks at it frequently.

(*In Romanian.*) Oh, my little darling! How are you??

Yes? Yes?

I miss you! I miss you too!

Thank you! What?

(*In English.*) Oh – in English! (*Covering the phone.*) She wants to talk to me in English!

Yes, darling, thank you. I am having a very lovely birthday.

What, now?

Oh... I am with a friend of mine.

What's that?

His name is Hendrix.

Yes. I know it's a funny name.

She says hello!

HENDRIX *waves.*

I wish I was with you though.

Yes it's okay. It's okay...

What?

(*Starts to get a little teary.*) Oh, I am selling ice creams!

No it's not hot here but the English people eat them all year round. The English people are a bit funny.

HENDRIX *laughs a little at this.*

How is school, my darling? Yes?

What?

LUMINITA *gets up and crosses the room,* HENDRIX *goes and sits on the bed.*

No, Claudia! Claudia, listen to me... I don't want you to do that. You must promise me you won't do that. Stay at home.

(*In Romanian.*) Stay at home with Mummy, darling, it's okay here but it's not really safe for a young girl like you.

(*In English.*) That's right. It's okay for me, but it's not okay for you, Claudia – okay? Okay?

I love you.

I love you.

I love you so much.

Is Mummy there?

You are on your own?

But you are okay, yes?

Okay, tell Mummy I will ring again.

(*In Romanian.*) I miss you more than anything in the world. I am very lonely without my little Claudia. Promise you will stay at home. Yes? I love you. I love you.

(*In English.*) I love you.

Okay, darling, bye bye. Bye bye.

She hangs up. She is facing away from the bed. She looks at the phone in silence for a long time. HENDRIX *stands up, awkwardly. Without turning around she hands the phone back to* HENDRIX. *He takes it.*

HENDRIX. Thanks. (*Beat.*) I bet that was nice.

LUMINITA *turns around quickly to face him.*

LUMINITA. What? Oh. Yes. Come on then, Hendrix.

She drops to her knees and starts to undo his trousers again.

HENDRIX. What are you doing?

She tries to get them undone. Becoming frustrated, she stops suddenly and begins to cry. She grabs HENDRIX *around the legs and buries her face into his stomach. She sobs her heart out. He stands awkwardly. He tries to come down to her level and help her up, but she pulls away from him and turns away. On all fours she cries.*

LUMINITA. CLAUDIA! CLAUDIA!

(*In Romanian.*) I want my little sister! I want to go home!

(*In English.*) I want to go home!

HENDRIX *kneels next to her, and manages to grab hold of her. She cries in his arms. Lights fade.*

Scene Three

KATIE *sits perched on the top of the sofa, seething. Her white shirt is covered with red paint. She has been drinking; there is a bottle of red on the coffee table with two thirds gone, and a glass. She hears* HILARY *and* HENDRIX *coming in and prepares herself. Throughout the scene she varies between white-hot rage and being incredibly upset.*

HILARY (*coming in*). But to say that to *me*! Shout it, rather. It's disgusting.

HENDRIX. I've told you to wait round the corner!

HILARY. Okay, okay, but still... (*Sees* KATIE.) Hello, love. Oh, paint. This is a good sign!

She goes to kiss her.

KATIE. Don't touch me.

Beat. Both HILARY *and* HENDRIX *are shocked.*

HILARY. What's the matter, Katie?

KATIE. You said you weren't in touch. You said she was out of your life.

HILARY. What are you talking about?

KATIE *retrieves a crumpled postcard from her bra. She reads.*

KATIE. 'Thinking of you and missing you both. It was pitch black in Nam at night and I couldn't see my hand in front of my face. Scary! But you know... *bon courage* and all that.'

HENDRIX. MEG!

He runs towards KATIE *to grab it. She pulls it away and then tears it in half and throws it behind the sofa. He runs to retrieve it.*

HILARY. Katie, it means nothing.

KATIE. No, Hils, I'll tell you what means nothing. *This* means nothing. Our *House*. Our *Life*. Our *Home*. Our *Family*. (*Begins to cry.*) You promised me that it was over. Now I can never trust you again.

HILARY. You're being ridiculous, it's just a postcard.

HENDRIX has sat down at the table and has pieced it together.

HENDRIX. Fuck! She's at Superbike in Holland – !

HILARY. Hendrix.

KATIE. And Hendrix hates me.

HILARY. He doesn't.

HENDRIX. She's met the Kawasaki team!

KATIE. Fuck you both. Fuck the three of you.

HILARY. Katie!

KATIE. I'm going to my bedroom. Don't try to follow me, Hilary.

HILARY moves towards her.

HILARY. Katie love…

KATIE. DON'T!

She leaves with a little sob. Beat. HILARY stands, shocked.

HENDRIX (*not listening*). She's been on the road for six weeks, camping out and staying in hostels and stuff. (*Beat.*) Mum, you were right! She says she just needed some head space. And she missed me and she thought about me every day. There's an email address! Have we got any Sellotape? This is so fucking cool.

HILARY. Jesus. Why now?

HENDRIX. She said she thought about you in Anne Frank's house.

HILARY. Oh for God's sake. Sentimental old cow.

She pours herself a glass of wine and drinks. He looks at her.

HENDRIX. Mother, Meg lived with us for seven years. She's biking across the world and we haven't heard from her for months – are you not the slightest bit interested in what she's been up to? Shit! She rode a Ducati Desmo 350. 1976, baby!

HILARY (*snapping*). Oh give it a fucking rest, Hendrix!

HILARY storms out. HENDRIX is left looking at the postcard. Even her snapping cannot break his spirit.

Scene Four

LEKO *strides into the room.* LUMINITA *is slumped up against the wall, her eyes closed. She seems a little fucked.*

LEKO. Luminita!

LUMINITA (*sitting up*). Yes?

LEKO. Why are you sitting there?

LUMINITA. I was just resting.

LEKO. Why are you not resting on the bed?

LUMINITA. I was just resting my eyes. I'm okay.

LEKO. You've done your cleaning?

LUMINITA. Yes.

LEKO. Are you clean?

LUMINITA. Yes.

LEKO. Good, the stud is here. (*Beat.*) Come here.

She gets up, a little wobbly, and walks over to him. He takes her chin in his hand.

I gave you too much gear, did I?

LUMINITA. Maybe a little.

LEKO. No more today. Look at me. Wake up.

He slaps her on the cheek, not hard, but enough to shake her a little.

Okay.

*He goes. She goes to the end of the bed, and under the duvet
is a can of Tyskie, which she drinks from and then hides
again. She straightens herself up.* LEKO *re-enters with*
HENDRIX. HENDRIX *is carrying a bottle of water.*

LEKO. Look who we got, Lumi. How you doing, stud?

HENDRIX. I'm okay thanks.

LEKO. Luminita says that you are a very good fuck.

HENDRIX. Oh. Well. (*Beat.*) Thanks.

LEKO. You like my cousin's spicy wings?

HENDRIX. Yes, very nice.

LEKO. After, you want to try a thigh?

HENDRIX. Yes okay.

LEKO. Good boy. Get him a beer, Lumi. (*To* HENDRIX.) Look
after my baby, okay?

HENDRIX. I will.

LEKO *goes.*

Luminita – are you okay?

LUMINITA. Yes I am very fine. You want a beer?

HENDRIX. No, I'm okay.

LUMINITA *stumbles off-balance slightly.*

What's wrong with you?

LUMINITA. I feel… I feel a little bit funny.

*He takes her by both shoulders, he helps her over to the
chair.*

HENDRIX. Sit down. You look really pale.

LUMINITA. I haven't been sleeping. I have this nightmare and
then I wake up. I – I've drunk too many beers and Leko has
given me too much to smoke.

HENDRIX. Well, smoking shouldn't make you like this. Oh,
hang on. Do you mean weed?

LUMINITA. Ah, Hendrix. You are just a child really, aren't you? Look at your lovely face. What are you doing here? In my room. What are you doing here? With me.

HENDRIX. Luminita, I'm worried about you.

LUMINITA *looks at him for a moment, and then laughs. He smiles.* HENDRIX *reaches in his pocket and pulls out an apple. He shows it to her and then he puts it by the bed. She laughs. He takes an orange out of his pocket and shows it to her, and then puts it by the bed. She laughs. He then takes his mobile phone out of his pocket and shows it to her. She doesn't laugh.*

Fully charged.

She looks at it like a reformed addict might look at their once beloved drug of choice.

LUMINITA. Not today. Thank you.

HENDRIX. Okay.

He goes to sit down on the bed.

LUMINITA. Don't! Don't sit there.

HENDRIX. Why?

Beat.

LUMINITA. I'm so ashamed.

HENDRIX. What?

LUMINITA. I wet the bed. (*Beat.*) Please don't tell Leko.

HENDRIX. Of course. Of course I won't.

LUMINITA. When he finds out he will go mad.

HENDRIX. I won't tell him.

LUMINITA. He will know. He will see.

Beat.

HENDRIX. Say it was me.

LUMINITA. *You* wet the bed?

HENDRIX. Say I spilt a beer.

LUMINITA. It will smell.

HENDRIX. Well, we can say I spilt my water. Pass me that bottle.

She does.

Do you have a sponge or a cloth?

LUMINITA. In the box under the bed.

He gets out a sponge and finds some antibacterial spray. He pulls the duvet back.

I'm so embarrassed.

HENDRIX. Don't be. It's fine. Look, here, I'll spill the water, spray it with this and then dab it. It'll dry in no time. It'll be clean.

LUMINITA. I can do it.

She gets up but stumbles. He goes to help her, and settles her back on the seat.

HENDRIX. Let me.

He pours water on the bed, sprays the spray and begins to dab the sheet with a sponge. She remains on the chair, watching him.

I was a bedwetter. (*Beat.*) What was your dream about?

LUMINITA. It was about me and my mother and my sister.

HENDRIX. Claudia?

LUMINITA. Yes! And my aunties and my grandmother and girl cousins. The little ones were running round. And we were drinking coffee, and talking and laughing. And we were eating tomatoes. Then I started to notice little things, like you know the coloured bit in your eye?

HENDRIX. Yeah.

LUMINITA. Well, none of the women had the coloured bit. It was all black. Like a big black circle. And their skin was yellow and hard when you touched it. Like wax. Then I looked at the little ones, and they all had breasts. Big breasts. Even Claudia. And Claudia was lifting up her skirt and I saw between her legs... was hair. And then we weren't eating tomatoes after all. We were eating chicken. (*Laughing a little*.) Fried chicken.

HENDRIX. That's pretty nuts.

LUMINITA. Then I was by the sea. I was on the beach, and next to me there was an old black horse. A sweet old black horse with a cartoon mouth and teeth. And I petted it. And with the horse was a man, I think it might have been Leko. He was nice and he helped me get up on the horse, and we walked down the beach in the sun.

HENDRIX. That sounds nice.

LUMINITA. There was a girl selling ice creams. The man got me down off the horse and bought me an ice cream. And I ate it and I watched as the man went over to the horse.

She looks at HENDRIX. *By now he has finished with the sheet and is sitting listening to her.*

HENDRIX. Go on.

LUMINITA. And he grabbed it by its cock. And he was pulling at it, and the horse was up on its back legs and spitting and the horse's cock was huge. Like a giant. And then the man called to me and I knew he was going to make the horse fuck me and then I woke up and I was pissing.

Pause.

HENDRIX. That's a fucked-up dream.

She nods.

This is clean now.

LUMINITA. Thank you.

Beat. HENDRIX *gathers strength.*

HENDRIX. Luminita. You need to leave.

LUMINITA. What?

HENDRIX. I think you should go home. Look, I understand you must really need the money –

LUMINITA. I don't make any *money*, Hendrix!

HENDRIX. What do you mean?

LUMINITA (*glances to the door, and then quietly*). Nothing. Forget it.

HENDRIX. I've been thinking about it. I'm going to help you. If it's money you need for a flight home, I can get it.

LUMINITA. No, Hendrix, it's not what I need –

HENDRIX. I mean I know you're here illegally but I'm sure we could work something out –

LUMINITA. NO!

She gets up and walks away from him. She gets two beers out. She holds one out to him. He shakes his head. She opens hers. She takes a long swig. She turns to him.

Look at me, Hendrix. Don't you want to touch me? Touch me.

HENDRIX. No. No, not like this. Listen to me, Luminita –

LUMINITA. Even if I could go home, what would I do when I was there? What would they think of me when they know all the things I have done? My mother, she wouldn't want to look at me. I wouldn't let Claudia near me. I would stink the place out.

HENDRIX. No!

LUMINITA. YES, Hendrix!

HENDRIX. Why did you come here in the first place?

LUMINITA. I am from Moldova. We have NOTHING. London is a big place where I am from.

HENDRIX. But to come here and do… this – !

LUMINITA (*angry*). NO! I thought I was coming to work in a club. To dance, yes. To strip, yes. But not this. Not this.

Beat. The penny drops.

HENDRIX. Oh my God, you mean…

LUMINITA. What?

HENDRIX. I know what you're talking about. We learnt about it in Politics.

LUMINITA. Did you? Did you learn about it in your classroom, Hendrix?

HENDRIX (*quietly*). Yes. Trafficking.

Beat.

LUMINITA. You know what? I think I have decided what I want to study at university. I would like to study to become a vet. It would be nice to see animals every day. Animals, and no more people.

Beat.

HENDRIX. We need to go to the police.

LUMINITA. NO!

HENDRIX. We have to – !

LUMINITA. Police are corrupt!

HENDRIX. Not all police!

LUMINITA. Oh, Hendrix. (*Strokes his face, kindly.*) Grow up.

HENDRIX. Okay. We won't go to the police. But I'll sneak you out. You can stay with me and my mum will help you get a flight.

LUMINITA. I can't!

HENDRIX. Why?

LUMINITA. He'll kill me! He'll kill my family!

HENDRIX. I can't believe that.

LUMINITA. WHAT THE FUCK WOULD YOU KNOW ABOUT IT?

Beat. Suddenly she glances towards the door, worried she has been too loud.

HENDRIX. Are you still here alone?

LUMINITA. Yes. The other girl who used to be here, Mimi, he sold her. Because she was very sick. She had AIDS. So he sold her for half of what he paid.

HENDRIX. Oh God!

LUMINITA. Hendrix, I have to protect Claudia. Promise you won't say anything to anyone, Hendrix, *promise*!

HENDRIX. You can't just stay here for ever!

LUMINITA. I can! Promise!

Beat.

HENDRIX. Okay. (*Beat.*) Where is Mimi now?

LUMINITA. She's dead, of course.

HENDRIX. Oh God.

LUMINITA *is crouching down next to* HENDRIX.

LUMINITA. You know what has happened here? I have made a bad bad bad decision. And now I have to pay for it. That is all. It is the way of the world. Do you understand?

HENDRIX *looks at* LUMINITA.

HENDRIX. Fuck.

Lights fade.

Scene Five

It is the middle of the night. HILARY is asleep on the sofa. HENDRIX creeps in and switches a lamp on. There is a half-empty bottle of red on the coffee table and a glass with dregs in. HILARY starts to stir. HENDRIX, in T-shirt and boxers, perches on the end of the sofa next to her. They speak quietly.

HENDRIX. Mum!

HILARY. God what is it? Is it Katie?

HENDRIX. No.

HILARY. Oh thank God.

HENDRIX. She's stopped the crying. And the banging.

HILARY. What time is it, Hen?

HENDRIX. It's after two. I can't sleep. (*Beat.*) I wanted to talk to you.

HILARY, in her half-asleep slumber is still pleased to hear this and rouses herself.

HILARY. Did you? Do you? Okay. That's great. You can speak to me about anything, champ.

HENDRIX, knowing he is taking liberties, reaches over, takes the bottle and adds to the dregs in his mum's glass. He drinks from it, looking at her. She shakes her head but chooses to ignore it. A warm moment between them.

HENDRIX. I wanted to ask you something.

HILARY. Is it about sex?

HENDRIX. No! God no. Mother, you know you've got a one-track mind!

HILARY. Okay. Okay. Sorry. Go on.

Beat.

HENDRIX. Say if I had a friend. And they were in trouble.

HILARY. What sort of trouble?

HENDRIX. Mum, please will you let me speak? Say I had a friend, and they were in trouble. And I thought there was

something I could do to help them. To save them, basically.
And it was going to be hard. Risky even.

HILARY. Dangerous?

HENDRIX. No. No, not dangerous exactly. Just... difficult. Big.

HILARY. Right.

HENDRIX. And it might involve them staying here for a little
while. And perhaps it might involve a little bit of money. But
I'll pay you back every penny – I'll come and work in the
shop – I'll do the veg display. But say we could really do
something, to help this person and make their lives better.
Because everyone deserves a chance, right?

HILARY. Yes.

HENDRIX. Everyone deserves to live a safe and happy life.
Right?

HILARY. Absolutely.

HENDRIX. Would you help me?

Beat.

HILARY. I'd love to hear some more about it, Hendrix, so I can
understand. So I can really / help.

HENDRIX. No I can't, Mum. Not now.

You just have to trust me.

Beat.

HILARY. Do you know what I think, Hendrix?

HENDRIX. What?

HILARY. I think you are a very beautiful young man.

HENDRIX. I'm not.

HILARY. You are. And of course. Of course I'll help you.

HENDRIX. That's brilliant. Thanks, Mum.

He smiles at her, takes a sip of his wine. A noise coming from
HILARY *and* KATIE*'s bedroom. They both jump a little,*

look in that direction and wait for a moment – suspense. No more noise. HILARY *reaches for the wine and takes it.*

HILARY. Give me some of that.

HENDRIX (*whispering*). How long do you think she's going to be like this?

HILARY. God knows, Hen. My nerves are shot to shit.

They look at each other and begin to giggle.

Scene Six

LUMINITA*'s room.* LUMINITA *sits on the edge of the bed.* LEKO *stands on the chair fixing a video camera to the wall.* LUMINITA *watches him, concerned. She gets up, and walks over towards him and stands patiently behind* LEKO.

LUMINITA. Please may I ask what you are doing?

LEKO. You may.

LUMINITA. What are you doing?

He gets down from the chair and admires his work.

LEKO. You are going to be a movie star, Lumi.

She looks at him, puzzled.

I set this camera up so now you can be a star.

LUMINITA. Oh.

LEKO. So now me and my cousin can sit downstairs and watch you getting fucked while we eat our chicken.

LUMINITA. Oh.

LEKO. You like the sound of that, little chicken?

Beat. LEKO *sniffs.*

LUMINITA. Yes.

LEKO. I thought you would. Come here.

She goes to him. He kisses her, with a strange tenderness and passion.

Get me a beer, Luminita.

She gets him a beer. He moves the chair to the centre of the room. He sits on it. She kneels down, a couple of feet away from him. LEKO cracks his beer.

I'm fucked, Lumi. Fucked. You know that?

LUMINITA. You are tired?

LEKO. Yes. I am hot and tired. We need some rain. And we need to sleep more. We haven't slept for days, have we?

LUMINITA. Not really.

LEKO. Too much fucking coke. It's not fair of me, to keep you awake. It's just I get lonely without you. Would you like to go to sleep, Lumi?

LUMINITA. It would be nice. Some time.

LEKO. Ah. Look at my little Luminita. My little chicken! You are so sweet sitting there! You would do anything I asked you to, wouldn't you?

LUMINITA. Yes.

LEKO. You would bark like a dog if I told you to, wouldn't you?

LUMINITA. Yes.

LEKO. Bark like a dog.

Beat.

LUMINITA. Woof.

LEKO. With more feeling, Lumi!

LUMINITA. WOOF!

LEKO. Be a dog, Luminita!

She gets on all fours and lets out a much more convincing woof.

That's good. You know my mother had a dog called Mitzi. When I was little. I might start to call you Mitzi. What do you think?

LUMINITA. I don't care what I am called.

LEKO. You don't *care*?

LUMINITA. I mean I don't mind.

LEKO. Okay. Maybe not. (*Beat. Sniffs and looks at her.*) Do you know what I love about you, Lumi? It's that you are beautiful and there is nothing going on behind your eyes. Men want to break you like a china doll. You are beautiful but you are empty.

Beat.

LUMINITA. Thank you.

LEKO. And you are mine. (*Beat.*) Luminita, what do you think of the stud?

LUMINITA. What do you mean?

LEKO. What do you think of him? Do you think he is a good guy?

LUMINITA. He's okay.

LEKO. I came up here, after he left yesterday. There was no condom.

LUMINITA. What?

LEKO. I looked in your bin. There was no condom.

LUMINITA. Maybe he took it with him.

LEKO (*laughing*). Come on, Lumi!

LUMINITA. Maybe he didn't use one! I don't remember!

LEKO. He needs to pay more for that. Do I need to kick his arse?

LUMINITA. No!

LEKO (*stands up*). He's a funny motherfucker. He's nervous, all the time. I walked past this door two or three times yesterday. All I could hear was you talking. Does he like to talk while he fucks?

LUMINITA. Yes! It helps him to relax!

LEKO. And he likes you to talk back?

LUMINITA. Yes.

LEKO. Did he bring you the fruit?

LUMINITA. Yes.

LEKO. Don't you like my cousin's chicken?

LUMINITA. Yes –

LEKO. Are you an ungrateful motherfucker?

LUMINITA. No – I –

LEKO. Are you an ungrateful motherfucker??

LUMINITA. Yes.

Beat.

LEKO. If something strange is going on do you know how upset I'm going to be, Lumi?

LUMINITA. There is nothing. I promise.

LEKO. Well, we'll be able to see it all now, won't we? (*Points to the camera.*) We'll be able to see what kind of a tiny little cock he's got.

LUMINITA. Yes.

Beat.

LEKO. If you ever try and leave me, Lumi, it would break my heart. You know that?

LUMINITA. I would never.

LEKO. You might. You might try. But if you do I know where I can get another girl just like you. You know, Lumi, in Moldova there is a little town called Soroca. And in Soroca is a street called Ismali. And at 47 Ismali Street lives a girl called Claudia. She is nine. But she looks older. More like twelve or thirteen. I will go and fetch Claudia, bring her here to England, and I will show her all the things her big sister used to do –

LUMINITA. NO! PLEASE, LEKO – !

LEKO (*not listening to her*). But maybe one day I will be fucking her and I will start to think about you and I will look down and I will just smash in her fucking face with my fist just because I miss you so much. Because you would break my heart, Luminita. (*Beat.*) So don't break my heart, Luminita. You understand?

LUMINITA. I understand.

LEKO. Good.

Beat. He drains the last of his can and puts it on the floor next to him.

Scene Six to Seven transition:

Very early morning. HILARY *asleep on the sofa.* KATIE *comes in wearing her fave jumper. She has been crying. She goes to* HILARY, *lifts the blanket, gets under and cuddles up to her.* HILARY *kisses her, relieved, and they both close their eyes. Time passes (they have been asleep a couple of hours).* HENDRIX *enters from the bedroom, with school rucksack over shoulder. He sees them. Beat. He leaves. As he leaves we can clearly see the word 'GAY' written in Tipp-Ex on his bag.*

Scene Seven

Lights up. LUMINITA *is sitting on the edge of the bed, nervous. The door opens and* LEKO *strides in with* HENDRIX *behind him.* HENDRIX *has come straight from school but has removed his tie and blazer and shirt and wears a T-shirt.*

LEKO. Okay?

LUMINITA. Okay.

  LEKO *leaves and slams the door. She looks at* HENDRIX *anxiously for a moment.*

HENDRIX. Hello.

  HENDRIX *has his back to the camera.*

LUMINITA. I need you to help me.

HENDRIX. Good! That's why I'm here! What do you want me to do?

LUMINITA. Come here to me and don't turn around.

HENDRIX. What do you mean?

LUMINITA. Just do it. Please!

  HENDRIX *walks over to her.*

Put your arms around me. Kiss my neck. Make it look like you really mean it.

HENDRIX. I don't understand –

LUMINITA. Please just come here!

  She peels his T-shirt off.

Take my top off.

HENDRIX. I – I can't!

  LUMINITA *sighs and takes off her own top. She grabs him. Holds him close to her and whispers.*

LUMINITA. Please. He's watching me. He's watching me all the time now.

HENDRIX. Where? I don't get it.

He looks around behind him, she grabs the back of his head. She peels off her knickers and throws them on the floor.

LUMINITA. Give me your hand.

She grabs his hand and puts it up her denim skirt, between her legs. She holds it there for a moment and then begins to move it back and forth. She makes noises to try to convince him she is enjoying it.

HENDRIX. Fucking hell!

LUMINITA. It's okay. Just be normal.

HENDRIX. This isn't normal!

Beat. She continues.

Luminita, this isn't right!

LUMINITA. Shh! It's okay. Now sit down.

She sits him down on the bed. She kneels down in front of him and starts to undo his flies.

HENDRIX. Luminita, what are you doing?

LUMINITA. Don't you want to get what you paid for?

HENDRIX. NO! Not like this!

LUMINITA. Come *on*, Hendrix.

HENDRIX. I – I want you to stop.

She comes up in front of him and puts her hands on his face, bringing it close to her so it can't be seen by the camera.

LUMINITA. He's watching me. We need to do it, and we need to make it look real.

HENDRIX. I can't!

LUMINITA. Think about all those dirty things you told me.

She gets his cock out of his trousers.

HENDRIX. Oh God!

She begins wanking him.

This isn't right!

LUMINITA. You want to pull my hair? Hey? Here…

She grabs his hand and puts it on the back of her head.

Go on! Pull it!

HENDRIX. No – I – Oh shit…

He takes his hand away. She grabs it and puts it on her bra. She continues to wank him.

LUMINITA. Okay? You like that?

HENDRIX. Oh God.

She reaches under the bed with one hand and pulls out the small plastic box with the condoms in. She takes it in one hand, rips the packet with her teeth and super-efficiently puts it on him.

LUMINITA. Okay, Hendrix.

She climbs on top of him and puts him inside her.

HENDRIX. Oh. Oh *Fuck*.

LUMINITA. It's okay.

Her eye meets his eye, close, for a moment. Then she begins to move up and down on him, eleven or maybe twelve times. HENDRIX lets out a gasp. It is over. LUMINITA stops moving and is still, head down. A moment of stillness together, they both breathe heavily. She gets off him, and with the same super-efficiency she pulls the condom off him and makes sure it goes in the bin under the bed. She stands a few feet away and sort of hovers. HENDRIX readjusts so he is covered.

Long pause.

HENDRIX. Why did you do that?

LUMINITA. I have to. There is a camera now. (*Beat.*) You want a beer?

HENDRIX does not answer. He stays still, head down. LUMINITA puts her knickers and vest back on. She picks up his T-shirt and gently throws it towards him. He does not catch it. He has not moved. HENDRIX quietly begins to cry.

Hendrix?

He cries. She is horrified. LUMINITA *positions herself as best she can between* HENDRIX *and the camera. She glances nervously over her shoulder at it.*

LUMINITA. Why are you crying? Don't cry.

He continues to cry, putting his head in his hands.

Don't! Don't cry, what's the matter with you?

Stop it! Stop it! (*Beat.*) Hendrix!

Stop being such a stupid little boy!

HENDRIX *jumps up.*

HENDRIX. FUCK YOU!

He grabs his T-shirt and bag and exits, slamming the door. She stands stock-still for a moment, then turns around and looks at the camera. She turns quickly and walks towards the window. She throws the curtains open, the room is flooded with light. She tries to open it. It has been locked. She cries in frustration. She tries again and again. Desperate, she throws herself against it several times. She sort of slides down the window, and onto the bed. LEKO *opens the door and watches her. Lights fade.*

Scene Eight

KATIE *is lying on* HENDRIX*'s bed watching television. She is wearing a short nightie. She is bored, stretched out across the bed with her head hanging off it, upside down. She changes channels listlessly. She settles on a channel – Rihanna's 'Rude Boy' is playing, she turns it up. The door slams. She sits up.*

KATIE. Hen?

HENDRIX *staggers into the room. He is carrying a can of Tyskie and is pissed and upset. It is raining outside. He is soaking wet.* KATIE *kneels up.*

Hennie!

HENDRIX. Get out!

KATIE. You're pissed!

HENDRIX. Yes! Yes… I'm… pissed. It makes a change from you and Mother!

KATIE. And you're bloody soaking!

HENDRIX (*mocking her accent*). It's bloody raining.

KATIE. Are you okay?

HENDRIX. Yes. Now get the fuck out of my room and leave me alone.

KATIE. Babes, what's happened?

HENDRIX. Don't call me babes, Katie, I HATE it!

KATIE. Have you broken up with your girlfriend?

HENDRIX. What do you mean?

KATIE. Come on, Hen. You've been out late loads recently! Is she a good fuck?

HENDRIX. God! You're so inappropriate!

KATIE. What? We're mates aren't we – ?

HENDRIX. NO. We're not mates! We're most definitely not mates. (*Beat.*) I'm moving out of here.

He gets a bag out of the wardrobe and begins to chuck random bits of clothing in.

KATIE. Don't be silly, Hen.

HENDRIX. No. No I am. I HATE it here!

He begins to get upset. He throws the bag down.

KATIE. Shhh. Sit down. I'm sorry, Hen. Talk to me.

She tries to help him sit down but he shrugs her off. He sits on the edge of the bed and drinks the last of his can.

HENDRIX. I'm a cunt.

KATIE. What are you talking about? You're not a cunt! You're lovely.

HENDRIX. HA! That's bollocks, Katie, that's really really bullshit.

KATIE. Believe me. I've known some cunts. You don't have it in you.

HENDRIX (*not listening*). Anyway… Maybe I don't wanna be lovely any more. Maybe Hendrix doesn't wanna be lovely… Any more.

KATIE. Well, I think it's tough shit because you are.

HENDRIX (*not listening*). Maybe Hendrix wants to be a cunt. (*Burps.*) Where's Mother?

KATIE. At a charity dinner. AIDS. Or asylum seekers. One or the other. Have you been crying?

She strokes his face. He pulls away.

HENDRIX. GET OFF ME!

KATIE. Is it the boys from school again – ?

HENDRIX. NO –

KATIE. Hils doesn't understand but I do!

HENDRIX. Right. That's it.

He jumps up. KATIE jumps up too. HENDRIX gently but firmly takes KATIE by the shoulders and moves her towards the door. She giggles a little and pushes back towards him.

KATIE. Is this you putting your foot down, Hen – ?

HENDRIX. Just leave me alone – !

KATIE. I can help you if you tell me!

HENDRIX (*looks* KATIE *up and down*). Bloody hell, Kate. Do you ever wear any proper clothes?

KATIE (*laughing*). What?

HENDRIX. Seriously. I can't remember the last time I saw you fully dressed.

KATIE. You like looking at me though, don't you?

Beat. Something inside HENDRIX *snaps. He pushes her up against the wall.*

HENDRIX. WHAT THE FUCK DO YOU WANT FROM ME, KATIE?

He grabs her breast with one hand and with the other he grabs and squeezes her face.

IS THIS IT? IS THIS WHAT YOU WANT?

KATIE. What are you doing?

HENDRIX. OR IS IT THIS?

He thrusts his hands between her legs.

KATIE. Hendrix!

He pulls his hand away and stumbles backwards, overcome with shame. He leans over, hands on knees, panting.

HENDRIX. Oh God. Oh God.

HILARY *appears in the doorway.*

HILARY. What the hell is going on, kids?

KATIE. Hennie's drunk. He's upset. He – he tried to kiss me. I don't think he meant it.

HENDRIX *picks up the bedside table and throws it.*

HENDRIX. ARRRGGH!

HILARY. Hendrix, stop! Katie, go in the other room!

KATIE. I don't want to leave you!

HILARY. GO. Get a glass of water.

HILARY goes to HENDRIX and grabs both his wrists.

Hendrix, stop this right now!

He flings her off and she falls backwards. HENDRIX continues to trash the room, ripping posters down, throwing bedding around.

KATIE re-enters with a glass of water.

KATIE. Here.

HILARY. Stop it! STOP!

HENDRIX. ARRGGHH!

HILARY. Please stop! Darling – have a drink of water!

HENDRIX. SHOVE IT UP YOUR CUNT, MOTHER!

He continues to trash the room. KATIE and HILARY back away into the doorway. Lights fade. Lights come up on LUMINITA's room. She is hurriedly packing stuff into large striped laundry bags. LEKO is taking down the video camera. LUMINITA takes the sheets off the bed and stuffs them in the bags. She runs to the door with the bags. She looks back and around quickly to see if she has left anything.

LEKO. Move, motherfucker!

He kicks her up the arse. She leaves. He takes one look around and leaves, leaving the door open.

Lights up on HENDRIX. He picks up the telly and throws it across the room. He drops to the floor for a moment. The sound of sirens outside. He runs out of the room.

Lights up on LUMINITA's room. There is shouting downstairs. HENDRIX's voice, and another with a strong Albanian accent.

VOICE. There is nobody up there!

HENDRIX. Luminita! I need to find Luminita – !

VOICE. No Luminita! *Nobody!* Gone! All gone!

HENDRIX. I need to go up there. I need to see!

He runs into the room and looks around. There is nothing. He takes it in. He sinks to the floor, crouching, exhausted, and puts his head in his hands. The voice, aggressive, from downstairs, shouting in Albanian, gets closer, as though coming up the stairs. Lights fade on him.

Scene Nine

HENDRIX *sits at the table. He has a bloody lip and a ripped T-shirt. There is a glass of water on the table.* HILARY *stands to the side of him, looking at him. Hands on hips. Pause.* HILARY *breathes in and out deeply.*

HILARY. Do you want to tell me what happened?

Beat. He does not look at her.

HENDRIX. No.

Beat.

HILARY. Where did you get the fat lip?

HENDRIX. I had a fight with an Albanian chicken man.

HILARY. Are you serious?

HENDRIX. Yeah.

Beat. He turns to her for the first time.

And do you know what, Mother?

HILARY. What?

HENDRIX. I broke his fucking nose.

HILARY. Really?

Beat.

HENDRIX. No. Not really.

Beat.

HILARY. I don't know what the hell you were playing at –

HENDRIX. I wasn't playing –

HILARY. I didn't bring you up to behave like that.

HENDRIX *laughs a little. Beat.*

HENDRIX. Why did you call the police, Mum?

HILARY. It was as much for your own safety as for me and Katie.

HENDRIX *snorts.*

You were physically violent towards us both, Hen. I don't know if you remember.

HENDRIX. I remember.

Beat.

HILARY. Katie's in pieces. She hasn't stopped crying all night.

HENDRIX. So what's new?

HILARY. I know things have been difficult. But Katie loves you. We both do. But you were like a madman last night. It was very traumatic.

HENDRIX. Where is she?

HILARY. She's in the studio.

HENDRIX *stands up.*

HENDRIX. I don't *EVER* want to see her again.

Beat. HILARY *is shocked by his directness.*

HILARY. Well, that's not going to be possible I'm afraid. Katie lives here with us.

HENDRIX. I'm going to say this to you once, Mother. Katie winds me up. Do you understand? SHE. WINDS. ME. UP. What are you going to do about it?

Beat.

HILARY. What do you suggest I do about it?

HENDRIX. Make her leave.

HILARY. I'm not going to make her leave.

HENDRIX. You made Meg leave – !

HILARY. If I made her leave, would it make things okay again between you and me?

Beat.

HENDRIX. Maybe yes. Maybe no.

HILARY. Well. Either way. Katie stays.

HENDRIX. That's your final decision?

HILARY. Yes. It is. (*Beat.*) You need a happy mum, don't you? You won't be happy if I'm not happy.

She goes to put her hand on his shoulder. He pulls away.

HENDRIX. Don't touch me.

Beat. HILARY *is shocked by this.*

HILARY. Hendrix, you know I love you.

HENDRIX. SO?

HILARY. What?

HENDRIX. So What?

HILARY. I tell you all the time, don't I? I love you. You're loved.

HENDRIX. So what? 'I love you.' *I love you I love you I love you.* That's not going to teach me how to be a good man, is it, Mother?

Beat. HILARY *is baffled by this.*

IS IT?

KATIE *appears in the doorway.*

KATIE. Hen?

HENDRIX. AND *YOU* CAN FUCK OFF!

KATIE. Jesus – !

HILARY. Leave it now, Katie, darling, go in your studio, I'll come in and see you in a minute.

Beat. KATIE *leaves.* HILARY *looks at* HENDRIX, *totally confused. He looks ahead.*

I'm *baffled* by this behaviour, Hen. Is this drugs?

HENDRIX (*scoffs*). Yes, Mother. That's the problem. I'm a heroin addict.

HILARY. Is this about the friend then, the one who needed help?

Beat.

HENDRIX. There is no friend.

This perplexes HILARY *further. She tries to sit next to him. She tries to rub his back. He pulls away.*

HILARY. I've made an appointment for you to see a child therapist. I know you're not really a child, but I thought we could start with that and then see where we go. She comes into the shop and she's very forward-thinking. I think you've been under an incredible amount of stress and it's taken its toll. We all need a little help sometimes, God knows I know that.

HENDRIX *puts his head in his hands.*

And, dude, I thought we could make an appointment with the head of Tafford Hall. Or Twickenham College, even, if you were happier finishing your A levels there. How does that sound?

Beat.

HENDRIX. Can I ask you a question?

HILARY. Of course.

HENDRIX. What did you think when I was born?

Beat. HILARY *thinks about this and gets a little teary.*

HILARY. We thought what a perfect perfect little person. We couldn't get enough of you. Natasha held you while they cut the cord. Even then we were planning. All the places we were going to take you. The things that you would see and

learn. We knew you were going to be a changer. We were
determined to raise someone who was the very best of
humanity.

HENDRIX. I'm not your project, Mother. I'm a human being!

HILARY. I know that, Hen...

HENDRIX. And even if I was – you haven't finished me yet!

HILARY. Okay. Calm down, Hendrix. Calm down. (*Beat*.) So
immediately after you were born, they lay you on my bare
chest, skin to skin. I looked down and I could see even then
what an exceptional person you were going to be. All dark
eyes and red-faced and screaming. Impassioned from the
word go. (*Beat*.) It was funny, because for the first few
minutes we thought you were a girl.

HENDRIX. What?

HILARY. Yeah it must have been the way they lay you on me.
We couldn't see you properly. But then Natasha picked you
up and cradled you in her arms. And then we looked down.

HENDRIX. And then what?

HILARY. And then we laughed.

HENDRIX. *Why??*

HILARY. Because we couldn't believe how stupid we'd been.
Darling, what's this all about?

Beat.

HENDRIX. Mother, have you ever heard of *ÜBER-
ADRENALINE-FEST?*

HILARY. No.

HENDRIX. Do you want to know what it is?

Beat.

HILARY. Yes, okay.

HENDRIX. It's a four-day motorbike festival in Germany.
Thirty thousand bikers. Riding and racing. Without their
helmets sometimes. And there's meat. Lots and lots of meat.
And women walk around in PVC bikinis.

HILARY. Jesus Christ.

HENDRIX. Yeah. And there's heavy metal. And strippers. Yeah, every night strippers taking their clothes off to heavy metal music and men shouting and whistling. And there's testosterone, Mother. Fields and fields of testosterone.

HILARY. Sounds idyllic, Hendrix.

HENDRIX. It's dirty and loud and it stinks.

HILARY. And your point is?

HENDRIX. I'm going there.

Beat.

HILARY. I don't think you are, love.

HENDRIX. Yep!

HILARY. What? On your own?

HENDRIX. No. Meg's there.

Beat.

HILARY. You're not serious, Hendrix.

HENDRIX. I'm going to ride with her. Do Europe for a bit.

Beat.

HILARY. And what does Meg have to say about this?

HENDRIX. She doesn't know yet. It's a surprise.

HILARY. She won't be prepared for you, Hen. She won't want you there!

HENDRIX. Fuck you, Mum! She will want me!

HILARY. You can't go. I'm still responsible for you!

HENDRIX. You've got Katie to look after now.

HILARY. Hendrix, this is madness.

HENDRIX *puts his hand on his mother's hand for a moment and looks into her face.*

HENDRIX. You've let me down, Mother.

He gets up and exits to his room, without looking back.
HILARY *is left grappling...*

Lights fade.

Closing scenes:

Lights fade up on a new room. There is no window. There is just a bed, and two of the large washing bags – still packed.
LUMINITA *sits on the edge of the bed, a large bruise on the side of her face. She is eating the remains of a doner kebab. She licks her fingers in between.*

Lights up on HENDRIX, *getting into a train carriage with a large rucksack. He looks around, checks his ticket, checks his pockets and sits down.*

LUMINITA *finishes the kebab, wraps it up in the paper and puts it in the bin. She gets a beer out from underneath the bed.*

HENDRIX *puts his rucksack under his seat and gets his MP3-player out of his pocket. He puts both earphones in and chooses a track.*

LUMINITA *cracks the beer and takes a long sip. She puts it down. She puts one hand on her chest and breathes deeply, to quell the nausea. Her other hand joins it. She settles herself. Then she moves her hands up to her neck. She grips her neck tightly for a few seconds and squeezes as hard as she can.*

HENDRIX *opens the top window on the train.*

LUMINITA *lets go and stares into space.*

HENDRIX *sits down. Takes a deep breath, leans his head back.*

LUMINITA *and* HENDRIX *both close their eyes. They both rock ever so slightly in the same rhythm,* HENDRIX *to the movement of the train,* LUMINITA *for comfort.*

Lights fade.

End.